CW01024405

The End of It

BRUCE FELLOWS

The Book Guild Ltd

First published in Great Britain in 2024 by
The Book Guild Ltd
Unit E2 Airfield Business Park,
Harrison Road, Market Harborough,
Leicestershire. LE16 7UL
Tel: 0116 2792299
www.bookguild.co.uk
Email: info@bookguild.co.uk
Twitter: @bookguild

Typeset in 11pt Minion Pro

Printed on FSC accredited paper
Printed and bound in Great Britain by 4edge Limited

ISBN 978 1916668 102

British Library Cataloguing in Publication Data.
A catalogue record for this book is available from the British Library.

For Sue

1

Chopsticks

A shot rings out.

Heinecke staggers back clutching his stomach before he falls to the deck and curls up, groaning. Jochen takes the gun from Gerda's hand and steps over to Heinecke. From three or four centimetres, he fires into Heinecke's forehead and the groaning stops.

Jochen opens his eyes. A woman is at the window, looking out. Standing there, she blocks the sun and is little more than a silhouette.

'Was that shooting, nurse?' he calls.

'Jochen.' The figure's turned.

'Lotte!'

'I dropped my lipstick, that's all.' She sits on the bed and takes his hand. 'You must have been dreaming. You've slept so long, darling. I didn't want to wake you.'

'What are you doing here? What about your children?'

She stands to take off her coat. She lays it over the

bed rail at his feet and turns back. On her breast, her little badge with the swastika, the League of Nazi Women Teachers or whatever it's called, catches the light.

'The headmaster's teaching them.'

'Oh.' He sighs. 'Leave me, Lotte.'

'Do you want to sleep?'

'I mean, I release you. Find someone who can dance.' He waves his hand towards his legs encased in plaster from feet to thighs. 'You can't stay with a cripple.'

She laughs. 'A few months and you'll be as good as new.'

From somewhere in the building comes the sound of a piano. *Chopsticks!*

'There he goes again! If you want to be useful, find that piano and slam the lid on the guy's fingers!'

She laughs again and leans over and kisses his lips. 'Is that better?'

'Yes, fully recovered now.'

Her face crumples. 'I don't think you're pleased to see me, are you?'

No! Is she going to cry? 'Lotte! It's just… oh, look at me!'

'I have been. You're a wonderful sight.'

With his legs like this, he can't roll over away from her, so he turns his face to the wall but that immediately makes his head spin, so he turns it back. Whoever it is is still murdering *Chopsticks*.

'You're miserable. I understand, stuck in bed. But just think how lucky you are to be alive. From what Major Winter wrote to your mother, it seemed like a miracle.'

'I came to in time to open the parachute, if that's a miracle. How long are you staying in Munich?'

'I'll need to go back late tomorrow.'

Another whole day! She's good to look at, though. That smile, the hair. He notices something.

'That badge wasn't silver before, was it?'

'I'm regional organiser now. Have you got any messages for your mother?'

He sighs. 'Tell her I'm fine. Tell her not to worry.'

'She will though.'

'I know. But what can I do? Tell her it wasn't my fault.'

'Of course, it wasn't.' She smiles. 'You're the best one there.'

Her teasing doesn't entertain him. He closes his eyes. Can he pretend to fall asleep? Feign a headache? Though with a fractured skull he doesn't really need to feign one. He sends her out to rustle up tea.

Silence. For an instant. *Chopsticks* lingers on though, always close to death but always fighting back. He wants to scream. What can he do about Lotte? He's got months of recovery to go. Learning to walk again. It'll be physical hell and, if she's always around, mental hell, too. And every time he goes to sleep the man that he and Gerda killed turns up. He's killed so many, why does only Heinecke return? Of course, the others were just machines he was killing, aiming at engines, hoping for smoke and flames and a man under a silk canopy high above the desert. But he held that pistol almost against Heinecke's head, heard him groaning, fighting for life as hard as *Chopsticks* is now, heard the groaning cease as he heard the shot. Anyone would think he's sorry he shot him, the Nazi shit!

Chopsticks stops. He waits for it to start again, waits and waits and then it does, but this time properly. Once straight through and then silence, apart from the normal hospital sounds: footsteps in the corridor, a laugh, low voices, the squeak of a trolley wheel. Heaven.

He was thinking something. What was it?

He wakes. Lotte's by the window again.

'It's a long way to come to stare out of a window.'

She turns.

'You found the piano?'

She nods. 'I played it through for him and then asked him to stop. He said he wouldn't disturb you for the world. The fruits of fame!'

'Huh.'

The librarian leaves a book from her trolley while he sleeps: *Goethe, the Collected Works*. Goebbels would love a picture of him reading it: the scholar warrior. It's heavy; heavy enough. Flat on his back in bed, he raises it vertically from his shoulder. Fifteen times he manages with the right hand. Fifteen more with the left. His biceps are aching. He's pleased; flying a 109 is a physical business, he'll need his strong arms back. He starts on his stomach muscles, sitting up and only slightly pushing his hands down on the bed. It's a strain but that's good, too. It barely affects his head, just a little dizziness that he's able to deal with and it goes away when he lies back. He does five repetitions of five sit ups and relaxes, exhausted.

There's another letter from Lotte on his bedside table. One a week since her visit. It's unopened. He's not ready for it yet. While it's unread, he can keep her shut away.

There's one from Bubi, too, torn open and read immediately. It brought his good fortune to the front of his mind. He's as lucky as Lotte said he was. He should be dead. Seven lives German cats have, and that was his seventh he escaped with. Perhaps he's really an English cat and has nine lives. He's worked out what happened. As he fell from the cockpit of his burning Gustav, the fin struck his head and knocked him cold. Naturally. But he was high enough to have a long fall building up to a horrifying speed until his eyes finally opened and he saw the desert hurtling up at him. He had just enough sense to yank the cord. He remembers seeming to stop dead in the air and the chute pulling him right way up but leaving him swinging so his legs smashed against the rocky ground almost instantaneously at such a speed that they each shattered in several places, and he collapsed helpless and unconscious again. It was the pain of being dragged by the wind in his chute across the rough and rocky terrain that brought him round again. By then, he's learnt, Bubi had found a spot to put his Gustav down, wheels up, and was running after him to collapse the chute and keep him safe until the doc got out to him. He really should be dead and would be, even after all his good fortune, but for Bubi.

The unit's back in Germany, Bubi says. That means Rommel won't be in Africa much longer. Why would they bring his best fighter unit home otherwise?

5

Fresh from his regular morning tour of the hospital, the guy whose bed is opposite Jochen's swings in on his crutches. He stops at the end of Jochen's bed.

'Paulus has surrendered.'

'Surrendered? The Sixth Army?'

'Yeah.'

The guy sits on the side of his bed and swings his legs up. He puts his hands behind his head and stares up at the ceiling. He mutters, 'Jesus! My God!' And keeps repeating it.

He says nothing else. But what else is there to say? Stalingrad's gone! After all that fighting! After a year or more!

So, a German army can surrender. It's not just the French or the British. Hitler will be raging. And what about Goering? It's late morning, he'll be starting a gigantic early lunch. And surrendered to the Russians! Was the Sixth Army still in its summer uniforms? His father said there were no plans for winter kit. But that was eighteen months or more ago. They must have it by now, mustn't they?

They cut off his casts. The shears crunch down the length of his legs. He keeps up a chirpy commentary all through the procedure until the dreadful sight of his scarred, white and wasted legs confronts him and he's shocked into silence.

'Not too bad,' the doc says. 'They did a good job back in Africa.'

He's never been a great physical specimen, but... 'They're so thin,' he says.

'Bound to be. You haven't stirred for months. It'll all come back. Exercise. Physio. You'll be busy the next few weeks.'

It can't make things any worse, so he reads Lotte's letter. Family news. Her father's doing some new research. Her sister's nearly qualified. She saw his mother; very well. She thinks they should set a date if his recovery is progressing! Oh, God! It's downhill from there, degenerating into lovey-doveyness that might once have been exciting but is now just nauseating.

He writes back. He's matter of fact, gives information on his progress, exaggerates his headaches, the state of his legs, how weak he is generally, how far he's got to go. He despises himself as he skirts his feelings, dodges the main issue of how entirely he's changed in the way he thinks of her, and when he's turned over the page, manages to reach the bottom with space for nothing more than *Love, Jochen*. How can he tell her? He simply can't yet. He needs to be back on his feet, have some control over his life again. He seals the letter and lies back in despair.

A nurse massages his legs three times a day. She's quite violent. He grits his teeth. They issue him with crutches. He collapses a couple of times but soon joins Carl, the guy opposite, on his morning tour.

He finds the piano and plays for half an hour. People pop their heads in and smile. A *leutnant* with a burnt face limps in and sits.

'I'm sorry,' the guy says when Jochen stops. 'I'm the

one who was playing *Chopsticks*. I can see how irritating that must have been.'

'No, I'm sorry,' Jochen says. 'I was being a grouch.'

'I had to stop when your fiancée asked me to. She's very beautiful.'

'Yes,' Jochen says and puts out his hand. 'Jochen Murville.'

'I know,' the guy says, and takes the hand. 'Oskar Schmitt.'

Perhaps he could bring them together, Oskar and Lotte. The Schmitts.

Jochen plays him *Chopsticks* and then sits Oskar down next to him and starts teaching him. As Oskar's playing improves, Jochen's legs get stronger.

Spring. The air is fresher, windows are opened wider. In the gardens the daffodils blow about and he can meander slowly over the grass and limp along the paths. Oskar has a girl, and when she brings along a friend, Jochen joins them on an outing for beer and sausages.

The beer is forbidden, so they can't have too much. Many in the street look away when they see Oskar's burnt face but the girls look straight at him when they talk to him and Jochen likes them for it.

Winter, his CO, arrives with cigarettes and brandy. He's about to join the staff of *General des Fliegers* Galland. He's left the *Geschwader*. How can that be? Winter *is* the *Geschwader*. He knows everyone, he knows everything. He's universally respected. He's also the eternal referee between Jochen and Jonny Beck. And Jonny's in charge now.

'That's a mistake, boss,' he says.

'He's the next up. You know how it works, Jochen.'

'He's a Nazi.'

'Well, that's good. For some.'

'I'll request another unit.'

'He'll want you back. You make commanding officers look good.'

'I'd kill him.'

'You didn't manage it before.'

'Christof stopped me. Christof!'

Christof, the black British POW who arrived in camp one day, became Jochen's servant and friend, and who tackled him to the ground as Jochen ran at Jonny waving his pistol after Dietrich died.

'We couldn't bring him back with us. We'd never have managed to keep him safe here in Germany. Can you imagine it? A black British soldier attached to the Luftwaffe!'

'And?'

'I found a prison camp and handed him over. Not the one he came from. Said we'd found him wandering with sunstroke one day and got him back to normal.'

'And they bought it?'

'They weren't interested. Too many other worries. They were expecting orders any day to surrender to the British. Probably sent back home by now.'

'Gone.'

Winter laughs. 'The look on your face!' He pulls a slip of paper from a pocket and passes it over. 'His sister's address. That will always reach him eventually,' he says.

He remembers life in the desert: early mornings, the cold stinging a cheek, winding up the motor of his Emil to get warm, laughing with the lads.

'How are Hans and Jurg? Still doing their double act? Keeping some other poor sod in order?'

But Winter isn't smiling.

'What?'

'Jurg's fine.'

'Oh. Is Hans dead?'

'When we pulled out for Sicily. They tossed for it. Jurg went in the transport.'

'And Hans was in the back of a Gustav?'

Winter nods.

'Who was it?'

'Their new guy. Hoeppner. He was OK. Not you, obviously, but he was OK. Good pilot. Fitted in. Everyone liked him.'

'Was it his fault?'

Winter shrugs. 'We never saw them after they took off. Maybe he got bounced or got lost. We left before light for safety.'

Hans, jammed behind the pilot into the fuselage of the 109, half squatting, half lying, little light, little air, no way out except crawling over the pilot's seat, no parachute anyway, bullets through him if they were attacked, otherwise down in the drink and no way Hoeppner could get him out. Drowning in the dark in the metal fuselage, joining all the corpses in the Med.

'He was married.'

'I wrote. The office has got the address.'

'I feel ill,' Jochen says. He pulls the brandy out of his locker, levers the cork out and takes a swig. He offers it to Winter who shakes his head.

'Eighteen months Hans and Jurg kept me alive! The hours they worked!'

2

Schwarze Orchideen

Berlin has become cosmopolitan. Foreign languages seem to be the norm on the streets; so many that Jochen can't recognise them all. French and Italian and Spanish are easy and Polish he's heard before, too, but a couple of tall, blond-haired men he's behind for a while, who look so German – although if they were, they'd be in uniform – gabble away nineteen to the dozen and he doesn't understand a word. Danish? Norwegian? There's no Russian, of course, though once he could swear he's heard English and swings round as a very smart-looking couple pass him. It's just the music of English he can hear, though, if you can say music about English; the words aren't English, and he can't actually understand anything. Dutch?

Is this what London's like, with people from all over their Empire thronging the streets, jabbering away? Is Germany on its way to imitating Britain with its own sort of Empire, an Empire of newly conquered nations, with all those nations' go getters turning up at the centre of things in order to get on? Probably. And probably to get on by filling the positions vacated by Jews – becoming professors, lawyers, artists – occupying their houses, taking the Jews' places on trams, in restaurants, in cinemas, while the Jews themselves rock and sway together in trains en route to those camps to undergo the final solution, as those two officers called it, in the conversation he overheard at that party. If what the officers said can really be believed.

His legs are aching now. He stops on a terrace to rest them and orders coffee and a glass of water. He won't be returning to Africa. Rommel's back in Germany and his army has surrendered, Jochen's heard, three months ago; 120,000 men. The allies are in Sicily so he won't be going there, either. Maybe Italy. But how much longer will the Eyeties hang on? They've been completely useless all the way through, and now they're back in Italy they'll probably just slope off home to mama, every one of them.

Here, it's the height of summer; and warm. Women are in summer dresses and he enjoys the show as they parade by at a saunter. He puts his cap on the table to avoid having to acknowledge salutes and runs his hand through his hair. Too long for tomorrow. He doesn't care but there's bound to be someone there who'll say something. He rubs one shin and then the other and imagines the scars there inflamed by today's exercise. He pulls the next seat round with a toe and puts his feet up on it.

The coffee's vile. He lights a cigarette to take the taste away and glances up as he's thrown abruptly into shadow.

'Hauptmann Murville.'

A thin face, well-shaved, dark flat hair brushed back, a slim body, young enough to be in uniform but wearing a good suit, dark grey. Someone official; the government, the Gestapo?

'Forgive me. I recognised your face. Your photograph. It's everywhere.'

The man looks familiar somehow. 'Have we met?' Jochen says.

'No. But you know my brother, Anton Heinecke.'

The man at the bottom of the Baltic.

'Oh. How is he?'

'I wish I knew. He's missing.'

'In action? I thought…'

'Yes. A couple of medical issues preclude his serving.'

'That's what I thought.'

'He's often spoken of you.'

'Has he?'

'He was very upset to hear of your sister's death.'

Strange, since Heinecke was the murderous bastard who killed her.

'Yes. Oh, forgive me, Herr Heinecke, won't you join me?'

He moves his feet and brushes off the chair. 'I was just resting my legs for a few minutes.'

'Of course. Your injuries. I read of them.'

'You'd think there would be something better to put in the paper.'

Heinecke smiles. 'Your health is important to the Reich.'

Jochen calls the waiter over. 'Coffee, Herr Heinecke?'

'Thank you. And it's Georg.'

'Call me Jochen, then.'

'My brother's disappearance remains a mystery. It's quite disturbing.'

'How long is it?'

'About a year.'

Rather more actually, Jochen would say, since that evening that he put the Beretta to Heinecke's head and paid him back for the rape and murder of his beloved twin sister, Ilse, and Uwe and Herbert tipped the corpse in chains over the side of the fishing boat Gerda was escaping to Sweden in.

'Dear, dear. That's a long time.'

'My sister and my mother are very anxious. They fear he's dead.'

Good. A bonus. But how could that monster have a mother?

'That's terrible. Could it have been a raid?'

Heinecke shakes his head. 'We've toured the morgues, of course.'

He hopes they enjoyed the experience.

The coffee arrives. Heinecke sips at it.

'It's not very good, is it?'

'It never is,' Heinecke says. 'I don't suppose you remember anything of your meetings with Anton? Anything that struck you as unusual or strange at the time?'

Only everything about that disgusting creep.

'It was quite a while back.'

'Of course. And I'm sorry for disturbing your day like this. I've been meaning to try to contact you for some time, but with your injuries... well, I couldn't impose. But seeing you like this.'

Yes. It must be fate. Kismet, is that the word? But he's had enough of this conversation and he long ago made a promise that if he ever found himself talking to Heinecke's brother, he would be non-committal and keep it short. He doesn't want to let anything incriminating slip out.

'I really don't think I can help you. My contact with your brother's been limited, you know. And most of the time when he was seeing my sister, I was in Africa.'

'Hauptmann Murville?' A woman's voice. He turns and smiles. A blonde girl, quite pretty, and a friend, not quite so pretty. The blonde girl turns to the friend. 'You see. I told you it was him.'

'Yes, it's him,' he says.

The blonde girl giggles. 'Would you sign your picture for me, Hauptmann?'

He turns to excuse himself to Heinecke but his seat's empty. He sees Heinecke's back disappearing into the throng. Good.

'What's your name?'

The steps are almost invisible in the blackout. He runs his hand down the rail just in case he slips. No more broken legs! There's a dim blue bulb over the door at the bottom. An awning above it keeps the light from spreading upwards to any possible Tommy bomber overhead.

He opens the door and pushes through the curtain behind it as the door swings shut. Light, voices, laughter, heat, smoky fug and Otto expressionless at the piano, playing like an automaton. But he's not alone now, an equally expressionless drummer and saxophonist have been hired to join him.

Jochen gets a brandy at the bar and turns back towards the band as they finish the number. Otto's morose face rises as he glances up at the smattering of applause and nods his thanks, but then his eyes meet Jochen's, and a wide smile drives the morose look away. He says something to the others and they bounce into a lively rendition of *Komm mit nach Madeira*. Couples stand and are soon jigging around. Jochen finds himself grinning. Otto grins back.

'Buy you a drink, Hauptmann?' A deep voice, but it comes from someone wearing a dress. Dark, perfectly coiffed hair, bare shoulders that would look better covered, gnarled fingers holding the cigarette. Certainly no beauty. And a good age. A woman? A time traveller from Weimar days?

'I'm fine, thanks. But I should get you one.'

'No gallantry, this is not a gallant time. This war is not gallant.'

'Which one is?'

'Mine was not like this one.'

Two brandies have arrived.

'Prost.'

'Prost.'

The lady knocks hers back.

'Now we'll dance.'

She grabs his hand and leads him from the bar. The hand is not delicate. It's a strong grip and from close up the hair is clearly a wig.

The bouncy tune is over, and Otto's moved on to a tango. Jochen's always loved to tango.

'*Schwarze Orchideen*! I love it,' his partner says.

The complexion is not like any woman's he's ever seen. Heavy make-up can't quite disguise the shadow on the jaw. But Jochen refuses to be affronted. It'll be another tale to tell the guys over brandy; decadence survives in Berlin! He throws himself into the dance.

At the end, he bows.

'You dance well, Hauptmann.'

Jochen replies to the dress and not the jaw or the voice. 'And so do you, madame.'

'A gentleman.' A hand touches the Knight's Cross with Swords and Oak Leaves at his throat. 'And clearly gallant, too. Thank you.' She turns back to the bar.

Otto has stopped and Jochen goes over. They shake hands.

'How are the legs?'

Does the whole world know about his injuries?

'Good enough for the tango, thanks.'

'I saw. Willi tests people out with a dance. Especially soldiers. Wants to know if they've really got balls.'

'Willi. Wilhelmina or Wilhelm?'

'What do you think?'

'I'm surprised he gets away with it. There are people I know who'd just ship him off somewhere.'

'It's a sort of party night. Someone's birthday. Fancy dress allowed. There are a couple of women in tuxedos somewhere.'

'Even so.'

'Iron Cross First Class in the last one, so he says he can do what he likes. He says someone will beat him to death soon, though, and end his misery. Have you heard from our friend in Sweden?'

He smiles, remembers his exultation that final morning in the desert when the mail arrived.

'I got a card. "Greetings from Trelleborg". Dreary looking place.'

'Fishing boats?'

'Yes.'

'Uwe got sepia daffodils. He was pleased.'

'Any message?'

'She said she found the family. Said they're very kind.'

Jochen feels suddenly weak with relief. He falls into a chair.

'Too much tango?'

Jochen laughs. 'Maybe.' He realises he's had tension inside him for months. He's known Gerda is there in Sweden but hasn't known she's really safe, surviving successfully, living a life with that Jewish family Uwe knows who agreed to take her under their wing. Now he knows and the pressure's gone, the relief is absolute.

'No sign of the gangster,' Otto says.

'There wouldn't be.'

'No?'

Not from the bottom of the Baltic.

'No.'

'We had his brother in here some time back. Asked questions all around. There was nothing to say except that he came in from time to time.'

'I met him. Ran into him. Georg.'

'First name terms.'

'His idea.'

'Playing the good cop,' Otto says.

'Playing it. And not very well.'

Otto introduces him to the other musicians. Grey hair, white hair, lined faces, coughs from years of smoky dens like this one, old style tuxedos like Otto's; Barney and Erhard. Barney does the occasional vocal, Otto says. Jochen pulls up a stool and sits in after their break. He and Otto improvise around *Berlin Bleibt doch Berlin* and Barney does a verse or two at the end.

Jochen feels a little drunk, but he's only had two brandies. It's the news of Gerda that inebriates him. She's there. In Sweden. Doing something or other. He's only got to stay alive and he'll see her again. Unless she's met a Swede who's swept her off her feet. And staying alive isn't really an 'only' proposition. It means years, and God knows how many years, of dodging bullets from Spitfires and anything the Amis send over. The odds are still against him. And his seven German cat lives are gone. Perhaps he can officially apply for two more from the British.

'What are you smiling at?'

'Nothing, Otto.' It must have been the cat lives but it's too complicated to explain.

'Play us something,' Otto says.

He starts in on *Shoeshine Boy*, but when he starts to sing the lyric in English, Otto shakes his head at him.

'They won't like it,' he says.

An officer comes in and, before the door closes, they all hear the siren. An exodus begins as some decide a public shelter will be safer but others come in, clearly thinking, as Jochen does, that the club will be just as safe. It's in a basement and there's another exit at the rear, so they're unlikely to be trapped inside. Jochen wanders around, sits when people invite him to, talks about music, Munich, the British, of whom he's met a few, accepts compliments on his decorations and his playing, accepts drinks, all the time hugging to himself his new knowledge that Gerda is safe and probably happy. The room feels happy, too, despite the raid going on above, less like a night club, more like a real club where people who like each other congregate. But then a row erupts.

'Get away from me, you degenerate, you pervert!'

Jochen strides over. 'Guys, guys,' he says to the pair of infantry *leutnants* staring white-faced at Willi. The jaw is a couple of hours more shadowed, and the wig is listing.

'Come and have a drink.' He guides them to the bar and orders brandies. Jochen's rank and decorations have silenced them. 'Don't worry about my pal over there. He can't help it. Ex-infantry. Decorated for bravery. Both Crosses. But he was blown up in the Spring Offensive of '18.' It's a not-unlikely invention. 'That's the infantry for you!'

The night goes on. And the raid. The club would normally have closed but it stays open. The band stops. Jochen takes over. Plays some Chopin, bits and pieces of Schubert, Beethoven. Barney stretches out on three chairs and goes to sleep. In the kitchen, Willi knocks up omelettes. With his dress on but his wig off, his straight hair, grey and brushed back, makes an incongruous figure of him. Jochen's omelette is good.

'Thanks, Willi.'

'My pleasure, Hauptmann.'

'Jochen, please.'

'Jochen. And thanks for the help. But I was looking forward to laying out that noisy bastard who was doing all the shouting.'

Jochen smiles. 'I thought they might need some protection.'

He leaves as light is just beginning. Willi accompanies him in a grey suit, having changed in the toilet. His drag is in a haversack over his shoulder.

'Daylight was no problem in the twenties,' Willi says. 'You could go out in the evening, walk home at dawn. You'd just get shouting and laughter but now... I don't mind a roughhouse, but they'd beat me unconscious and then I'd end up in a camp.'

'Why do you do it, then?' Jochen says.

'I can't help it. It's liberating. It's my nature.'

'Have you always been queer?'

'Bent? I'm not. Two sons. One in the army, one in the navy.'

'Does your wife know?'

'Yes. I'm ashamed to say it terrifies her.'

'Because something might happen?'

'I've told her to deny all knowledge of... my hobby, my condition. She's to feign disgust.'

Having been up all night, Jochen is limping.

'Have a rest,' Willi says. They stop. The air is smoky from the raid but there's no other evidence of it where they are. Perhaps the English bombed the fires that are usually lit in the nearby countryside to lure them away.

'Would you like me to ban you from flying?'

'What?'

'If you've had enough, I could get you grounded.'

'How?'

'Examine you. Write a declaration stating that your injuries render you incapable of wartime flying. We get lots of men through like you.'

Jochen stares at him.

'At the hospital. I'm a surgeon. Didn't you know?'

Jochen shakes his head.

'I thought Otto would have told you.'

'No.'

'Well, what do you think? You've done more than your share, haven't you? We could keep you alive for later.'

'Will there be a later?'

'There's always a later. I could see you this afternoon.' He gives Jochen the name of the hospital.

'I've got to be somewhere this afternoon.'

'Tomorrow.'

'Willi, if I'm not up there, they'll just send someone else. Some poor kid who's not nearly as good as me. I'd be as good as murdering him.'

They walk on.

'Anyway, you don't realise, I'm just dying to get up there again. What I need is a letter saying I'm completely fit to fly. You can write that for me if you like.'

Willi laughs. 'You're suffering from a condition much worse than mine and much more dangerous. Someone else can write that letter.'

The air's got smokier… no, dustier. Something stirs in his memory. The name of Willi's hospital.

'You must know my fiancée's father. He's based at your place.'

'What's his name?'

'Josef Hofmann.'

'Oh.'

Is there some shock in the exclamation?

They've reached a crossroads and there's rubble across the street to their right. Several buildings are down but there's no fire. He can smell and taste the dust in the air. People swarm all over the rubble. There are policemen trying to organise them.

They hurry down.

'What were you going to say about Dr Hofmann?'

'Later, Jochen. I'll be too busy now,' Willi says.

He sees Willi announce himself to a policeman and start examining the injured sitting and lying on the pavement. Nearby, a building has collapsed in a mound of bricks and concrete. Still wondering about Willi and Lotte's father, Jochen joins the line of people, mostly men, passing lumps of the rubble hand to hand from the top of the mound. A couple of men peer down at someone obviously inside, burrowing for survivors. The sky's clear and promises heat but the sun isn't up yet. The burrower shouts and the men above haul out a blonde-haired woman who appears uninjured but is certainly dead.

The mood of the rescuers is angry.

'Bastards!' People keep shouting. 'I wish I had one of them terror flyers here!'

'Look at that poor girl! What's she ever done to them?'

Another shout comes from behind Jochen, and he turns. Two men in labourers' clothes are holding a British airman between them, red hair, with blood down his face.

'Trying to hide he was, the bastard! But we sniffed him out, didn't we?' the man on the left says to his chum.

'We did.'

'Yeah, and I gave him one with this!' A third man following behind and carrying a bundled up parachute under one arm, brandishes a spade with the other. Several men have rushed forwards.

'String him up!'

'There's a lamp-post!'

Jochen drops his lump of rubble and clambers down the mound towards the men, yelling as he goes. 'Stop! Let him go!'

He understands the crowd's fury, their urge for revenge, but he can't stand by and witness a killing.

'Fuck off!' he hears. Many men surround the airman now, shouts of hate and fury all around. Jochen draws his revolver and fires into the air. The men turn to face him.

'You can't shoot us all.' A tall man at the front, white hair.

'No, but you'll be first,' Jochen says.

The man steps back. Some others look at each other, not sure now.

'Let him go! He's a prisoner. He must be interrogated.' He lays it on. 'He'll have important information for us.'

The crowd moves away a little. He spots a policeman dithering on the edge of the group.

'Officer, disperse these men at once!'

Finally having an instruction, the policeman, another elderly man, though suffering many resentful stares and comments, shoos them back to their rescue work.

'Don't we get a reward?' the man with the spade says.

'You've got his parachute, haven't you? Silk.'

He's left with the airman, a navigator by his brevet, with a Distinguished Flying Cross ribbon below.

'Thanks,' the man says in German.

'Do you speak German?'

'No,' he says after a moment, still in German.

Jochen speaks English. 'Do you have a pistol?'

'No.'

'Can you walk?'

'Yes.'

'Headache?'

'Yes.'

'The Luftwaffe is responsible for downed enemy airmen. Don't try to escape or I'll have to shoot you.'

'Escape? Where to?'

Jochen laughs. He's spotted a small hotel on the far corner of the crossroads. 'We'll go over there.' He looks round. There are many eyes on them still.

They wait for a horse and cart to pass and then weave

their way across the road between the bicycles of the early birds off to work. Two men in the uniforms of enemies with a gun between them. Quite bizarre in the middle of Berlin.

In the hotel he phones Luftwaffe HQ to arrange a pickup, then demands coffee and rolls for two, a bowl of warm water to bathe his prisoner's face, and a downstairs room to wait in. The Englishman's name is Richard Leonard, a flight lieutenant from Winchester, once capital of England, Jochen learns. Leonard is happy to give Jochen his address.

Walking home after he's handed over his prisoner, Jochen stops near another mound of rubble. An old man is trying to sell a few items that he's spread out along the pavement.

Jochen doesn't want either of the dirty old saucepans, nor the coat hanger or the candle stick, but there are a few records that he picks up to look through.

'I don't know how they survived,' the old man says. 'The gramophone's buried under that lot.' He gestures at the rubble. 'So I've got nothing to play them on now.'

It's a treasure trove: Caruso and then – joy! – Schubert and Beethoven! He laughs.

'You know this guy's a Jew, do you?' It's Schnabel playing on the Beethoven.

The man is mortified. 'No, sir, I didn't. Give me them back. I'll smash them.'

'No, I'll buy the lot.'

A car takes him the twenty-eight kilometres from Luftwaffe HQ Berlin to Rangsdorf airfield. On the hard standing there's a night fighter Junkers 88 with radar antennae all over the nose. Not far away is a Gustav. No sign of the pilots. When he comes out of the latrines, another Gustav is landing. It taxis up and Jochen watches the propeller windmill to a stop in the silence after the engine is cut. Lucky bastard, whoever he is, to have flown here. The hood swings up. The pilot clambers out. He grabs his cap from the space behind the seat and a bag from the hatch in the fuselage.

His heart sinks when the pilot turns and starts towards him. It's Krause. The man who threw him out of his *staffel* in France two years ago. He comes to attention and his salute is returned.

'Good morning, sir.'

'You're still a scruffy bastard, Murville.' Krause doesn't quite smile. 'But it looks like Winter found the good in you that I couldn't.'

In the bar, they find Rall, the pilot of the other Gustav, just flown in from Russia, and Prince zu Sayn-Wittgenstein, whose 88 it is outside.

'You're the Prince!' Jochen says when they're introduced. 'I've heard of you. How do I address you? Your Highness or something?'

'Sir's the usual thing, since I'm a major. Or as we're comrades, Heinrich will do.'

Later, in the Junkers transport, the night in Otto's club catches up with Jochen and he sleeps the three hours north to the airfield at Rastenburg. In the circuit to land they surely pass over their destination, the *Wolfschanze*, Hitler's eastern command centre, but it's well-hidden among trees and impossible to see.

Goering's limousine picks them up, swastika and Luftwaffe pennants fluttering on the wings, rain spattering on the shining black metal. They drive through three rings of security, each fenced with barbed wire, and each with a checkpoint to stop at. Armed guards examine their papers each time. Goering, as huge and ghastly as ever, greets them among the trees when they get out. He's grumpy.

'You're late!' he says. 'I've been waiting.'

They have to hand over their pistols at the door. Zu Sayn-Wittgenstein refuses, makes a fuss, says it's part of his uniform, and only desists when he notices they're all staring at him. In an anteroom, Goering shouts at the orderly, who's a second late in offering drinks.

When they've all got one, Goering disappears.

'What's up with Fatty?' Jochen whispers to Rall.

'He'll be all right when he's had a shot of whatever it is he sticks in himself.'

Three minutes later Goering's back, beaming. Jochen remembers this transformation from his previous meeting.

Goering gives Krause a playful punch on the arm and flicks his thumb at Jochen.

'How do you like your boy now, eh, Krause? Not done badly for a waste of space, has he?' He turns to Jochen and through a loud laugh says, 'He thought you were a waste of space, you know. Just a playboy.'

Jochen smiles. 'I probably was, sir.'

Krause smiles, too. Is all forgiven?

They eat. 'Just a snack,' Goering says, as they enter the dining room with its gleaming ranks of silver cutlery laid out on snow white napery.

Two hours later they're on coffee, cigars and cognac as Goering disappears again.

Jochen asks Rall about the Ivans he's fighting. There are lots of them. A few good pilots in a few good units. Mostly useless, he hears. They compare the American fighters they've each faced: Jochen, Tomahawks and Kittihawks; Rall, Airacobras. Not as good as 109s but, with the right pilot, as always…

Goering returns. 'Do up your buttons, he's ready.'

Goering leads them in to the Führer. Still a funny looking man, with that lock of hair and the Chaplin moustache. They line up. Jochen is the youngest and the lowest rank, but he's the last because his is the highest-ranking award. Krause and the Prince receive the Knight's Cross with Oak Leaves, Rall the Oak Leaves and Swords, which Jochen is already wearing. It's the Knight's Cross with Oak Leaves, Swords and Diamonds that Hitler hangs round Jochen's neck. Hitler's chosen the diamonds himself, he tells Jochen. He does that for all recipients of the Diamonds. Jochen stares ahead, keeping his nose out of range of Hitler's stinking breath.

They all sit with coffee, though Hitler doesn't partake. Hitler has a private conversation with each in turn. He asks Jochen about his family and surprises him with the knowledge he reveals: his sister's murder, his father's death in Russia, his engagement.

'You must marry soon, Murville. The Reich needs your babies.'

Then the Führer holds forth to the group. He's weird. He talks about railway lines in the east. In Russia? How the gauge will have to be changed to run German trains to the new villages and towns that will be built there, what a vast enterprise it will be. They all glance at each other. Stalingrad is lost, the Sixth Army is lost, Africa is lost, Sicily too. Now railway lines in Russia?

'But, excuse me,' Rall says, 'how long do you think the war will last? When we went into Russia, the papers said it would end by the first snows. Now the third year of snows is not so far off and we're still there.'

Will he be arrested? Shot?

The Führer looks at Rall in a kindly way. 'I can't tell you that. This might be an open area. We have our settlements here. When the enemy comes from the Asian steppe, we'll defend our homes as in the days of Genghis Khan. I see a deep valley, but I see a bright strip on the horizon. We are vastly increasing our production of tanks and fighters, as well as bringing millions more men into training. And we have weapons in development so powerful that I must keep them secret still. But I can tell you they will transform the course of the war overnight. Be assured, we will win.'

They all sit in silence for a few moments until an aide reminds the Führer of an imminent strategy meeting. He leaves them. They raise eyebrows at each other and then Goering comes in like a whirlwind.

'Good time, boys? Did he go on? He does that, you know. He imagines you all rush back and tell your guys what you've heard. He likes to spread his thoughts and ideas. Come and have a drink.'

They all start to leave.

'Can I see that?' he says, as Jochen's passing him. He pulls the ribbon of the Diamonds over Jochen's head. He stares at the gems with the eye of an expert and tuts his disapproval.

'Honestly! He's got a greengrocer's eye for diamonds. I wish he'd leave it to me. And these jewellers just rob him blind. I'll get you another one. With proper diamonds.'

He hands it back. Jochen is perplexed.

'What about this one?'

'Keep it. They're still diamonds, after all, even if inferior ones.'

In the car back to Rastenburg they're all silent with their thoughts. How are they managing to push up production so much? Where are the millions of men coming from? Does the man running Germany always behave like this? Is he superhuman, as they're all led to believe, or is he just delusional? And who is there around him who can bring him face to face with reality?

Night falls as they fly to Berlin and they all sleep. Krause and Rall will stay at Rangsdorf so they can return at first light to France and Russia respectively. They eat together and then the Prince borrows a *kübelwagen* that he can drive back to Rangsdorf later to collect his 88, and he and Jochen drive to Berlin. Jochen's told him about the club.

On the way, they talk with disbelief and horror about Hitler's ramblings. At the club, there's no Willi to test whether the Prince has the balls to dance with him. They chat to Otto and then Jochen plays *Schwarze Orchideen* for the tango enthusiasts. Halfway through, he remembers their arrival at the *Wolfschanze*.

'Why were you so keen to keep your pistol, Heinrich?' he says when he re-joins the Prince at the bar.

'I was going to shoot the crazy bastard guttersnipe.'

At the hospital he finds no sign of Willi or Lotte's father. While he waits, he flicks through old copies of *Luftwaffe*. He's in a couple of them. He studies his picture alongside those of other officers. Everyone calls him scruffy, but he can't see it.

In the consulting room, the doctor reads the notes Jochen's brought from the Munich hospital. Through the window he sees pigeons flapping in and out of a lime tree. The leaves are beginning to turn gold. It'll get chilly soon.

'Hauptmann, everything looks fine here but there are some checks I must do.'

Jochen says he's had no headaches or dizziness for ages and though his legs pain him after an hour or so's walking, otherwise there's nothing. The doctor shines a light in each eye, looks in his ears, puts a stethoscope to his chest and listens, asks him to stand on one leg for thirty seconds and then on the other. Finally, he sits him in a revolving chair, swings it round and stops it suddenly. As previously directed, Jochen stands and immediately walks to the door without swerving from the direct path.

The doctor ticks various places on a form, dates it and signs with a flourish. He takes the carbon copy for himself and passes the form and all the notes back to Jochen.

'There you are, Hauptmann. Fit to kill every one of those bastards up there.'

Free to fly again! But there's no excitement, only relief. And will he still be able to do it? There's anxiety in there somewhere, too. He hurries down flights of stairs and across a hall with the file of notes tucked under his arm. Outside he drops the notes in a bin and lights a cigarette as a noisy group of nurses emerges from another door. A couple of them catch his eye and laugh and wave. He waves back.

Now HQ. But another nurse comes out. Blonde hair dragged back tidily but emerging over her ears as if it was done many hours ago. She's clearly tired but it's the same face, though he didn't know she was a nurse.

'Hertha,' he calls, as he starts towards her.

'Jochen.' She smiles. 'Well, well.'

'Still the girl I was in love with at kindergarten.'

'You told all the girls that.'

They kiss on each cheek.

'I'm sorry about Ilse. I was going to write but...'

'Don't worry about it,' he says. 'When was it? That lunch in France? With Lilo? Nearly three years ago. Was that the last time we saw each other?'

'You'd landed on the beach. Did you get in trouble?'

'Terrible. But it's all forgotten now.'

'I can see.'

'Nursing!' He laughs. 'Where's Lilo?'

'Married; child; in the country with her in-laws.'

'Good.'

'Not really. He was at Stalingrad.'

'A prisoner?'

'We hope so.'

'Your guy?'

'Ulrich.'

'Yeah.'

'He was killed.'

'Oh, Hertha.'

They're silent for a moment.

'Walk me home. I'll make some coffee.'

But he must get to Luftwaffe HQ. He arranges to go round to Hertha's in the evening.

At HQ an *Oberst* tells him they'll have orders for him the day after tomorrow. Jochen's anxious to get in the air again. A phone call arranges everything for tomorrow at eight.

'Your *Geschwader*'s spread about around Wilhelmshaven at the moment to catch the heavy babies when they come over the coast,' the *Oberst* says.

'Major Beck?'

'Yes. He's keen to have you back, I hear.'

'I was due to have a *staffel*.'

'We know. Don't worry.'

He calls for Lotte. She has work to do, marking and so on, but she comes to Hertha's with him for an hour. Hertha's in a green dress. Her hair's down. She and Lotte are a German type. An Aryan dream. They get on well and sit together on a sofa with a pot of tea and they talk, he imagines, about him. He sits at the piano and plays *Schwarze Orchideen*. It's a strange little tune, nothing much really but it's got him caught for the present.

Hertha's father, General Deichmann, is in the Balkans, her mother in the country with Lilo and the child and the in-laws. Hertha has the place to herself and has asked a few people to meet Jochen: another nurse, a plainer girl called Ursula; a young doctor in uniform, a *leutnant*, currently attached to the hospital; a couple of neighbours, a bit older. They dance to the tunes Jochen plays for them, then he plays a Chopin prelude and straight afterwards *Lady Be Good* because American music makes Lotte anxious. He's rewarded with the scowl he expects and he grins back. He takes Lotte home then goes back to Hertha's. The neighbours have gone and the *leutnant* doctor leaves with Ursula to walk her home. Jochen and Hertha sit for an hour and talk about their youth, not so long ago, and their families. Jochen has tragedies to relate, Hertha too. Everyone in Germany has, of course.

When he wakes, it's three in the morning. As he's pulling on his clothes, Hertha stirs and turns to him. He puts on a light by the bed. She screws her eyes up, dazzled.

'Sorry,' he says about the light. 'I've got to go.'

'Have you?'

'I've got two planes to fly at eight o'clock.'

'At the same time?'

He laughs. 'Even I'm not that clever.'

He pushes a foot into a boot and pulls it up. 'I wouldn't be rushing off otherwise.'

'Good. I'm glad you came back,' she says.

'Yes.'

'I won't lay claim to you. Don't worry.'

'No.'

'You are a bastard, though, Jochen. Poor Lotte. She shouldn't be marrying you.'

'I don't imagine she will be.'

'What?'

'I don't think I can go through with it. She's a Nazi.'

'That badge thing? Is that it?'

'But she believes it all. Jews are evil, she thinks. She believes all that garbage. It sickens me.'

'Aren't you going to tell her?'

'I don't know how to. How will she take it?'

'Better than if you just leave her standing at the altar.'

Berlin-Adlerhof. The ME 108 is a sports plane really, seats for four, but he's on his own. He's forgotten nothing, of course. It's just like riding a bike. He goes up to three thousand metres. It handles like a 109 without the weight and the violence. It's gentler, kinder. He stunts around, makes the earth spin and twirl, makes it rush towards him and slowly move away, grow smaller, makes the earth and sky change places. He opens the throttle and tears along at, he checks carefully: three hundred kilometres per hour, slower than any of their bombers. He turns back after an hour, does half a dozen touch and goes and then lands in a 109 style three pointer. The sun comes out briefly and makes the cockpit suddenly hot through the canopy. This is a wonderful day, like a childhood birthday. He wants to shout and cheer, ride through town whooping and yelling like a cowboy in one of those Yank westerns, waving his hat and firing a pistol in the air.

He hands back the 108 and signs for the Storch. He's off

the ground in about forty or fifty metres and climbs slowly straight ahead. The airfield's disappeared behind him. The sky's overcast. He stops climbing at five hundred metres, meadows and trees below, different shades of green. Cows in the fields, like a child's picture. He feels like a bird; that's why pilots all love the Storch. Glass to the sides, glass above, with the wings attached on either side above him, no wing below to block the view. The view below, around, above, is superb. He moves the stick to the right and the earth beneath swings slowly round, the airfield emerges then moves to the left and leaves his view. He opens the throttle wide. After a minute or two the dial reads 175. He slows back to cruising; 130. He sails on, looking around, looking down at woods to the left.

Bang!

The plane shakes. The starboard wing drops. His eye turns automatically to the wing and he swings the stick left at once in reaction to the jagged hole he sees, just as a dark shape flashes past. As the Storch turns he follows the shape as it gets smaller to his right, then behind him and then through the glass on the left and then through the windscreen in front of him as he straightens up. The shape is turning in a wide circle. Olive drab, white stars, elliptical wings, blunt nose; Thunderbolt. He's seen them in photographs and recognition silhouettes. What's it doing here? Coming back for him, obviously. He sees flashes from the wings and puts the stick down and to the right. He dives in a curve as the Thunderbolt rockets by above him. He reaches the trees and flies along the side of the wood just below tree top height. The Ami is turning again. Before he's recognised it as an idea, Jochen pops the Storch up above the trees and flies on just over the tops. The Ami is turning quite a way above Jochen in order to dive on him. Jochen twists the Storch from side to side so that he can just keep the Thunderbolt in sight behind and he slows to just above the stall. He doesn't wait to see gun flashes but opens the throttle and puts the stick over to the left. He sees the trees to his right, where he was flying only moments ago, mashed by the bullets that are missing him. He's used up all his tricks. Now he'll land and run for it.

He cuts the engine and drops by the side of the wood. The Storch runs only a few metres before the long grass stops it. Before he can touch his straps, he sees the Thunderbolt smash into and through the trees and disappear amongst them. There must be the sound of snapping, falling trees but it's lost in the monstrous noise of the Thunderbolt's engine. Then there's silence for fifteen, twenty, thirty seconds? He's climbing through the door when he hears a crump and a whoosh and flames shoot up from the wood. He takes a few steps but stops at the edge of the trees. He can feel the heat from where he stands.

He stares into the wood where the flames are rising, flicking from side to side with the breeze, catching branches and setting them alight, about to consume trees that have stood there since they were shoots from acorns and seeds, a hundred years or more ago, and in the middle of it a man becoming a frazzled lump of meat.

The pilot must have got himself completely lost. Compass not working? Or shot up? No sun out to guide him? There were no signs of a raid in the area. All this way across an ocean to get lost and fly way beyond his normal range, but still with the will to shoot at a Nazi pig chanced upon when desperately searching for a landmark, tracking his eyes across the landscape and then across the map on his knees, darting eyes around outside for 109s and then ahead of him; a little plane with black crosses on the wings.

What a waste! He can't tell any relative of this man he saw his end. He has no idea who to tell. He stands there mesmerised by the scene. An ancient wood going up in flames. Tiny creatures in there scurrying for dear life. Then, twenty metres from him, pushing through the branches at the margin of the wood and staggering, a man! Brown leather flying jacket. Scorch marks down his trousers.

Jochen laughs. He waves. The man points a handgun. Still laughing, Jochen puts his hands up as the man approaches.

'Are we going to walk to England?' Jochen says in English. 'Do you know the way?'

The pilot stops, looks at his gun, takes it by the barrel and offers it to Jochen. He loves it at once, a Browning automatic.

'Can I have the belt, too?'

The man unbuckles it and passes it over.

'More bullets?'

The man rummages in a pocket on his leg and pulls out a small box. Jochen slips it into a tunic pocket, straps on the gun belt and slides the automatic into the holster.

'Billy the Kid!'

But the pilot isn't ready for jokes. Jochen offers a cigarette, lights it and they smoke together.

'How did you do that?' the American says after a while, in fluent German.

Jochen knows the accent. 'Are you from Berlin?'

'My grandparents. How did you get me to do that?'

'I was too low. You were too fast. I've seen it before, over the sea, over the desert. Guys just fly straight in. Can't judge the height. The trees. Like a carpet.'

'You're a fighter pilot, I guess.'

Jochen nods.

'How many have you got?'

'Some.'

'More than me.'

'How many have you got?'

'One.'

'More than you, then.'

Jochen puts out his hand. 'Jochen Murville. From Berlin.'

They shake hands.

'Sam Levine. From New York. Coney Island.'

'Samuel. Jewish?'

Levine doesn't answer.

There's a truck approaching from the airfield.

'Don't tell them. If they ask, pick a church and say you belong to that.'

Levine offers a cigarette. Lucky Strike. Pulls out a Zippo and lights them both.

'Here.' He holds the Zippo out to Jochen. 'Have this. I won't manage to keep it long, will I?'

Jochen spots Levine's watch. 'You won't keep that either.'

Levine unstraps it and passes it to Jochen.

'I'll bring them to New York when I visit. Afterwards,' Jochen says and hands Levine the packet of cigarettes from his pocket.

3

Una Furtiva Lagrima

Ice has formed on the inside of the canopy along the glazing bars. Jochen slaps his thighs to get some warmth into them. The radio crackles in his ears. The sky above is a rich blue.

Lower down, cotton wool clouds sail along over the countryside. Jochen spots the vapour trails coming in from the direction of the sea just as the first black bursts of flak appear around the silver dots at the head of the trails.

He calls into his oxygen mask. 'Heavy babies, ten o'clock. One thousand below.'

The *staffel* is flying northwest at nine thousand metres, twelve 109s against this American air fleet. The escorts will be up there somewhere but there's no time to worry about them, the bombers are much more important. They fly arranged in four carefully positioned vees of three to form solid boxes of twelve. The arcs of fire of the thirteen machine guns every Flying Fortress carries interlock to create an almost impenetrable screen around each box. Box after box after box is flying into Germany.

'Wide open!' he calls and pushes the throttle to full as he puts down the nose, aiming at the first of the Ami boxes, at the twelve bombers flying tight together. It won't take long at the seven hundred kilometres an hour the Gustavs are doing now. The bursts of flak around the bombers cease.

'Thunderbolts coming down,' a voice calls in his ears.

'Victor, victor,' he calls back in acknowledgement. Will they have time to attack before the escorts hit?

As he pulls the stick back to come out of the dive, he feels his weight treble and he's squashed down into his seat. He's flying level now, straight at the bombers. He closes the throttle a little to give him more shooting time. He'll have only seconds. He takes the leader. Getting him might have an effect on the box. The aeroplane ahead grows and grows, a giant silver whale glinting in the sun. Tracer bullets fly past him from the Fortress's front guns, two of the thirteen; heavy calibre, 17.9 mm. One hit is bad news, three or four will take him down. He fixes the bomber's nose in his sight and fires from, it must be, about six hundred metres. One thousand, he counts; the tracer from the front guns stops, two thousand; the glass in the gunner's position sparkles as it smashes, the pilot's windscreen, too, three thousand, he counts, and stops firing to pull the stick back and to the right as the whole nose of the Ami bomber, very close now, disintegrates and the machine rears up and collides with the bomber just behind and to its right. Then he's past and sees no more.

He climbs in a spiral. Looking down, he sees the two B17s locked together, going down in a spin until they separate. A wing falls off, a tail comes away and then parachutes begin to blossom white against the fields and woods kilometres below, one, two, three, four from the twenty men in the two machines. As his spiral continues, he loses his view.

He climbs away. A Thunderbolt flashes past tailed by a Gustav.

'Seven, break left,' he yells, and the Gustav turns at once, followed by the second Thunderbolt Jochen's spotted behind it.

He puts the stick over to the right to follow the pair. The Thunderbolt is turning behind the Gustav. A big mistake. Its strength is in the dive. Jochen puts the stick left and pulls hard, following the Thunderbolt in its turn and pushing himself into his seat. The Thunderbolt slides into sight and Jochen fires, one thousand, two thousand. Bits fly off the fuselage, the wing root, and smoke starts from the Thunderbolt's engine. More smoke, and the cockpit canopy goes. Jochen pulls a tight turn in the opposite direction to clear his tail. As he completes the turn, he sees the Thunderbolt below begin a spin and a trail of parachute becomes a deployed canopy.

'All clear, seven,' he calls, though he can't see the other Gustav now.

'Thanks, boss,' comes through the crackle in his headphones.

He pushes the stick down and aims the Gustav at the silver giants grinding on relentlessly below.

'Still there, Eric?'

'Yes, boss,' his wing-man calls. 'All clear at present.'

'Same again, then.'

He pulls out at the bombers' height and bores in. He cuts the throttle a little. Tracers come at him, whip past him and then there are heavy thumps in front of him, two, three, four, it seems. His speed cuts. A trail of smoke comes past the canopy. The propeller stops. He puts the nose straight down and switches off the engine.

'I'm hit. Breaking off.'

'Victor, victor,' he hears from Eric.

Nothing to see to the left or right as he goes down.

'Break left, boss!' He does at once, in time to see a Thunderbolt pass and Eric's Gustav fire at it and then bank left to follow Jochen.

He puts the nose down again, wishing he had an engine, but that's still trailing smoke. He's at four thousand metres and puts the stick right because he's been flying straight long enough. As he turns and the earth moves to his right, he sees a Gustav diving past with flames coming from the engine. He can't see the number. A shape tumbles from the cockpit.

'Eric!' he calls, but there's no answer. A glance up shows the boxes of silver aeroplanes flying on, though a couple of the bombers have turned back and are losing height with smoke coming from engines. A parachute has appeared where the Gustav's pilot should be.

He banks left now and twists to see what he can behind him. It seems clear. Where is he? He won't get home. The engine's still smoking but isn't burning.

Two thousand metres. Country below. A village or two. Lots of space to put down on. He doesn't want to jump again. He banks right and then left to see behind. Nothing.

One thousand. Where to go? He looks around. Starts on the left, swings his eyes in an arc.

An airfield! He knows it. He recognises the road and the nearby wood and the buildings, the layout of the hangars. Jever. *Geschwader* headquarters. Pre-war. Well set up. Proper quarters. He could have a shower. But don't count your chickens. He banks to left and right to check behind again before he lowers the under-carriage. He drops the flaps and lets the Gustav fly itself down on three points. There's still a trail of smoke from in front and he raises the hood to get out the moment the Gustav stops.

He leaves the machine with the guys who arrive to stop the smoke, grabs a lift in the accompanying *kübelwagen* and goes to find a telephone.

Bubi answers.

'I'm at Jever,' Jochen says. 'Who's not back?'

'Frohm, Woll, Geiger, Huwald, Rech and Schmidt.'

'Geiger jumped. I saw him. Chute opened.'

'Good.'

'I just want to have a word with Jonny and then I'll find some transport.'

'I'll come and get you.'

'No, stay by the phone so we know who's safe.'

Five guys gone possibly; probably seven Gustavs lost. Out of twelve that took off. At that rate, tomorrow will be their last day. How many Amis did they get? His two

Fortresses and a Thunderbolt; the two Fortresses he saw trailing smoke, say that's two more that don't get home. That's five for five. Equal. They need to get four or five to one; twenty, twenty-five Amis against their lost five.

They're towing his Gustav back. He stands in the door and watches as he lights a cigarette with Levine's zippo. What's Levine doing now? Underground, perhaps, tunnelling out of his camp. Allied airmen do it a lot, apparently. And then get caught. Jochen admires their attitude. Captured but not surrendered.

He walks over to the guy checking his Gustav.

'How bad?'

'You'll need a new engine, sir. And a propeller.'

'I'll speak to Oberst Beck,' Jochen says.

'I don't think he's back yet, sir.'

Jochen finds the office that says *Geschwader Commander* on the door. Dark green polished lino floor, dark polished desk, chairs, the Führer on the wall and Fatty next to him.

He sits and stares out of the window, seeing nothing. His *staffel* should be all down and refuelling, rearming, getting ready to hit the boxes again on their way back. Instead, half are missing and he's in the wrong place with no aeroplane. What a mess!

As usual recently, when he's been despondent his mind drifts on to Lotte. Why does he keep putting it off? He should just tell her. He knows that. Hertha knew it, too. She told him he was a bastard. She told him to tell Lotte. If he was this indecisive in the air, he'd be dead. In the air you have to act. There's no time for thought. Dive in, guns firing.

He must end it now! He must! But he hasn't got a reason that anyone he likes would really acknowledge. Some might agree it's a shame Lotte's a Nazi. But it's what you get these days. What can you expect? Years in the League of German Girls turns you into a Nazi. It's what the organisation is for. It's inevitable. Except the Hitler Youth failed with him.

What would his mother say? She isn't a Nazi. She helped him when he got Gerda to Sweden. But she thinks Lotte's a splendid young woman.

'Don't break her heart,' she'd said to him. And Lotte's heart will break when he tells her. He's taken her along on the ride. She believes she's part of his meteoric rise and, without kidding himself, that is truly the only correct description of his success: he's won every medal that the Reich has on offer; he attends parties at the Goebbels', he's had dinner with Fatty, private chinwags with Hitler.

It will break her heart all right.

What heart though? Has she got one? She believes all that repulsive garbage about Jews. How can she have a heart? But if he can dismiss her feelings like that, just with that thought, what kind of heart does *he* have? He'll be as bad as any Nazi.

But he can't have a life with her! He couldn't bear it, knowing she thinks like that. And pretty soon she wouldn't be able to bear *him* either. It would be one of those dreadful loveless marriages: two people tied together when they want to be separate, each barely able to tolerate the other's presence.

How will she react when he tells her, though? It will be awful. A tearful, possibly hysterical scene. And where will he tell her? Not when they're out somewhere. Not in public. She must be at home. They must be at her house. The house her father got from a Jew when he took the Jew's job.

Perhaps he could try the idea he had the other day. Could he? Why not? No. It's the coward's way. Well? That's him, obviously. No. But why not?

He focuses at the sound of a distant Gustav. Wheels down, it passes the window. Then another comes. He picks up Jonny's phone and asks for his airfield. Bubi answers again.

'Frohm and Rech are dead,' Bubi says. 'Huwald saw them go in. He's down at Twente.'

'Where's that?'

'Holland. Machine's OK, he's refuelling.'

'Any luck?'

'He got a Thunderbolt.'

'What about you?' Jochen says.

'A Fortress. It blew up. Horrible.'

'That's seven we got then.'

'Just a minute,' Bubi says and Jochen hears the phone put down, hears Bubi's voice, indecipherable at a distance, then clear in his ear again. 'Woll's back. He got a Fortress but Schmidt jumped.'

'Thanks, Bubi. Can you get off again?'

'Yeah. We've got five serviceable Gustavs. We'll be ready.'

That's eight they got then and only two dead. That's four to one. And only four Gustavs lost. But only six Fortresses gone from all those boxes still flying over Germany.

He stands up as Jonny comes in. Massive, tough, exhausted looking, bags under the eyes, but a smile. Or is it a grimace? Probably still thinking of the day Jochen tried to kill him in the desert.

'Jochen.'

'Jonny.'

'Need a ride home?'

'I do. My Gustav needs fixing, too.'

'Tomorrow. We'll send it back purring.'

Beck opens a filing cabinet, takes out brandy and two glasses. Jochen watches him pour, thinking how silly he looks in his riding breeches.

'If I'd known it was there, I'd have helped myself,' Jochen says.

'Prost.'

'Prost.'

'There's some coffee coming.'

'How many did your guys get?' Jochen says.

'Three so far. All Thunderbolts. There are four not back yet.'

'No bombers?'

Beck shakes his head.

'It's the desert all over again, Jonny. We're being overwhelmed. And getting too tied up with the fighters to hit the bombers.'

The coffee arrives.

'I was going to ring you but I'm here now.'

'Problem?'

'I need to ask your permission to marry.'

Beck laughs. 'Is that still a requirement?'

'It's in the book.'

'Permission granted.'

'Well, Jonny, the thing is, I want you to refuse.'

Beck laughs again. 'Trying to wriggle out?'

'I wanted to marry her but now I don't.'

'What's this poor girl done?'

'I can't marry her, Jonny. She's a Nazi.'

'National Socialist.'

'National Socialist.'

'You don't deserve her. Marrying a National Socialist would be a badge of honour for you. I'm a National Socialist.'

'Just say no. I'll send the application through, and you can reject it.'

'I'm not doing your dirty work for you. What reason could I give?'

'Say I'm not worthy of her.'

'You're not but it wouldn't wash upstairs.'

'Financial insecurity.'

'You're a *Hauptmann*! That's a pretty good screw.'

'I'm too young.'

'How old are you?'

'Twenty-three.'

'In your prime.'

'I'm immature.'

'The truth at last. But too subjective. I couldn't write that down.'

'Please.'

'Sir.'

'Please, sir.'

'Ha! You said it!'

'Well?'

'Grow up, Jochen! You should know better. Though it pains me to say this, you're the best of us, and you know it. They can't even get you when you're flying a Storch.'

'How do you know about that?'

'The story's all around the Luftwaffe. Everybody knows. 158 in the desert, how many now you're back home? How many Fortresses?'

'Two today, so that's nine. And two Liberators.'

'Thunderbolts? Lightnings? Mustangs?'

'I haven't seen a Mustang yet.'

'Lucky for them. The others?'

'Does it matter?'

'I want to know how far behind I am.'

'A Thunderbolt today, so that's six. And two Lightnings.'

'And you reported back…' Beck looks at his calendar. 'Three weeks ago tomorrow. He should give you another medal.'

'There isn't one. But while we're on medals, I want to put Bubi up for a Knight's Cross.'

'Fine. That's a proper request. Has he got fifty?'

'One today makes fifty.'

'Do the paperwork and send it along.'

'Bloody paperwork!'

'Get used to it. Hain's dead. I'm giving you his *gruppe* as of now. I'll send you along the…'

'Paperwork. I never thought I'd ever have a *gruppe*. Three *staffeln!* I didn't even have one *staffel* four weeks ago.'

'Your fiancée will be proud.'

Jochen laughs. 'Yes. Give Bubi my *staffel.*'

'Of course. Now get out.'

Two new guys report. Berger and Diesch. He takes them up early the next morning. It's cloudy with intermittent sun. He sends them off first and watches. Diesch tries to pull his Gustav off the ground too soon. He's lucky. The Gustav lifts a wing that threatens to flip the machine onto its back on the grass, which will very likely cause it to burst into flames. Diesch slows and gets the wheels back on the ground and then allows the Gustav to fly itself off. He and Berger have had thirty hours conversion to the Gustav. Jochen and his pals didn't have that much when they converted to the Friedrich, but they'd all been flying 109s for months or years before that. Berger and Diesch have come from basic training. One hundred hours total flying time. How can he take them up against the Amis with that?

He leads them up to nine thousand metres and tells them to follow him in line astern. He tells them each manoeuvre before leading them into it. He dives, and pulls up into a loop, but rolls out at the top then spirals down to the left, slows and banks into a tight right-hand turn and goes round twice.

'Shit,' he hears through the earphone crackle. Berger's voice. Through the right-hand side of his canopy, he sees a Gustav spinning towards the earth.

'Keep calm,' he calls, 'you've got lots of height.'

The spin goes on but finally he sees the Gustav straighten into a dive and eventually pull out.

'We'll come down to you,' Jochen calls and puts his nose down. 'We're going down, Diesch,' he calls. And, 'Still there?' when he gets no answer. 'Diesch?'

As he pulls up alongside Berger at five thousand metres, the sun glints off a silver dot far below them.

'Diesch!' he yells. 'Diesch, wake up!'

There's no response. A few seconds later there's the flash and smoke of an explosion in the corner of a field very near some farm buildings.

He's had enough. 'Berger,' he calls, 'we're going home.'

They enter the circuit at their airfield at Marx and let down on the grass side by side but fifty yards apart. Jochen pulls back the nose a few feet up to let the Gustav settle itself, but Berger attempts a wheeled landing with the tail up. He sails on across the field with the Gustav refusing to stop flying and settle.

'Open up!' Jochen yells. 'Go round again!'

Berger reaches the edge of the field and hits the hedge. The Gustav tips up on its nose and flips over on its back. If it burns, Berger's dead. Jochen taxis over and reaches the wreck just as the fire truck does. He climbs out and watches a man with an axe hack the canopy open so that Berger can crawl out. He stands. His face is white. He sees Jochen.

'I'm sorry, sir,' he says.

Jochen nods. But it's not Berger's fault. He shouldn't be here. He should be at a training school doing circuits and bumps and getting time in the air with something more forgiving than a Gustav.

'Come on,' he says to Berger, 'I'll get you a drink.' He leads the way to the truck for a ride back.

What happened to Diesch? Oxygen starvation? Or did he pull too tight a turn and pass out. He'll never know. One useless pilot left and two Gustavs gone.

He sends Berger off in the 108 they keep for getting about in, with orders to practise tight slow turns without falling into a spin or passing out and then do twenty minutes of three-point landings. It's not a 109 but he can get the technique right. If they get a report of a raid developing, Berger is to get on the ground at once so that no Thunderbolt can kill him.

'Believe it or not,' Jochen tells him, 'your life is precious.'

The day's turned really chilly. He rubs his arms as he walks back to his office.

There's a shout in a voice he knows well. 'Boss!'

He swings round and grins. In a greatcoat and carrying two large bags on his shoulders, Jurg is striding across the apron towards him. Jochen last saw him giving his canopy a final shine before he took off on that flight in the desert fourteen months ago, when his Gustav caught fire. A metre away Jurg drops the bags and comes to attention. They salute. Then they shake hands and Jochen slaps Jurg's arm two or three times.

'Let's get inside, I'm freezing,' he says.

'I've got just the thing for you then.' Jurg pulls a jacket out of one of his bags and passes it over; a brown leather flying jacket with a sheepskin lining and a white US Army Air Force star on a blue disc on the upper arm. 'It's loot, I suppose. I bought it off a guy in the mess.'

Jochen pulls it on as Jurg continues.

'If you don't want it, I'll sell it on again.'

But Jochen loves it and feels instantly warm.

In the office they drink coffee and talk about Hans, shot or drowned but anyway, dead in the sea.

'I wrote to his wife,' Jochen says. 'It won't do any good, of course.'

'She'll be pleased to have got it. From you. It'll mean something. He thought you were it. He'll have told her.'

They think for a moment.

'Thanks for getting me here,' Jurg says.

'I want to be properly looked after.'

'What about the last guy?'

'He was good but he's not you. He's promoted and got a new job so he's happy.'

Jurg will be in particular charge of the crews maintaining the Headquarters flight, Jochen, and three others, and will assist the officer responsible for engines in the *gruppe*.

He writes the recommendation for Bubi's Knight's Cross. He's pleased that Bubi's lived long enough for him to do this for him – the guy who saved his life. It's only a futile piece of junk to hang around his neck, of course, but it's the best there is and he'll be offered instant respect. And girls love the Knight's Cross. Jochen will be able to mock him about all the letters he'll get when the photos come out in magazines. Letters still arrive for Jochen. He has them sorted for anything with a Swedish stamp.

An envelope arrives from Beck, *Office of the Geschwader Commander* stamped in the corner and Beck's pencil scrawl across the back, *May all your troubles be little ones!* Jonny has expedited his permission to marry. The bastard!

Berger reports back. Jochen has watched a few of his landings. They've looked all right. A message comes in. Much activity detected in area Dora-Dora, the area on their charts over the North Sea, off East Anglia. The B17s will be climbing and forming up in those boxes of twelve with all the machines guns converging; the Thunderbolts heading up above them.

The pilots gather. His new jacket is the source of comment and admiration. Eric Geiger is still limping from his jump but insists he's fine to fly as Jochen's wing-man. They wait in their cockpits for a signal. Jochen sees Berger standing watching. They start their engines.

'Away you go,' he hears, and he leads them off, the three *staffeln* of the *gruppe*.

Thirty-one serviceable Gustavs out of thirty-six on the nominal roll. They climb to nine thousand and beyond. The altimeter needle goes as far as it can, but they've probably gone beyond that. His oxygen is working. The others should be checking too. He reminded them at the briefing. That may have been Diesch's downfall. Ice has formed inside the canopy as usual. There are many clouds below but up here the sky is dark blue.

'Vapour trails at twelve o'clock,' a voice calls.

There they are. Silver specks with white trails just appearing over Germany. Black bursts of flak dot the sky all around the glinting bombers.

'Follow me,' he calls and puts the nose down. He's seen no escorts yet and no one else has called them. The bombers get slowly larger. It's a head on attack and he aims for the centre of the pack. The rest of the *gruppe* spread out on either side so all can hit the bombers at the same time. He's lining up the lead bomber in his sight when Eric shouts.

'Jochen, break left!'

He does so without thinking and the Flying Fortresses are gone from his vision. He closes the throttle a little to tighten his turn and his arms grow almost too heavy to move. The bomber boxes appear above him and flashing darts of fighters chase each other, turning, diving, climbing. He turns to see behind him but, as usual in a Gustav, sees very little.

'Anything around, Eric?'

There's no answer. He climbs in a spiral that Thunderbolts find difficult to follow, aiming at the bombers that are ploughing on towards where? Wilhelmshaven? Hamburg? Before he can work out how to attack again, he spots a silver fighter coming at him from his one o'clock. He turns towards it and fires when it fills his sight. Flashes sparkle around the engine while tracers fly past his own cockpit. The Ami breaks to the right. Square wing tips, a square tailplane, a bulbous radiator on the underside of the fuselage. His first Mustang. He fires again. Splashes of light around the fuselage and wing roots. It's gone. Hit for sure. Back to England? Or just out of this fight to collect his thoughts?

A Gustav flashes by in flames. A shape tumbles out and falls. Jochen twists his head to watch as he resumes his spiral climb. The parachute streams out and then mushrooms.

He's still climbing when he spots a Mustang chasing a Gustav. He doesn't need to shout 'Break!' because the Gustav is twisting and turning like a mad thing. Jochen latches on behind the Mustang and on a right-hand turn eases it into his sight. He fires and gets hits on the tail and starboard wing. The Mustang puts its nose down at once and dives. Jochen follows but finds the Ami pulling away. Pulling away in a dive! It's a shock. Gustavs dive better than anything. But not any longer. He lets the Mustang go and climbs again. The Gustav is circling. He sees the number. It's from one of his new *staffeln* and he doesn't know who it is.

'All clear, Nine,' he calls.

He's still climbing to get above the Fortresses but then he spots the red fuel light. So soon! Those Mustangs have been around up here all the time he has, and they've flown from England and they have to get back there. How long can they stay up?

'Got to leave you, Nine.'

'I'm coming, too, boss.'

They put their noses down and dive for home. Get back quick, refuel and get back up again. They have to let down gently through the clouds that have gathered while they've been up, though, and by the time they're ready to go again, the sky is overcast and low, and rain is just starting. They're not equipped for this and hardly any of them are trained for foul weather flying. He stands them down and reports in to that effect.

Five minutes later he's called to the phone. It's the General and he's furious.

'Why aren't you up?'

'The weather, sir. It's raining.'

'It's raining? Frightened of getting wet? You've got hoods.'

'The visibility's awful, sir. We can barely see the other end of the field.'

'Too scared to fight them, are you? Is that what you want me to tell the Reichsmarschall?'

Tell him what you like, you stupid shit. How many of us do you want dead?

'I'll take that *gruppe* away from you!'

'Yes, sir.'

'Don't you "yes, sir" me.'

'No, sir.'

'Get up there now!'

'That's a direct order, is it, sir?'

'Of course, it is, Murville!'

He puts the phone down and tells Backhaus of his HQ flight to get the *staffel* together. The other two *staffeln* are based in separate buildings. Geiger hasn't returned or phoned. Perhaps he was the one who jumped from the blazing Gustav. The guys wander in. There are nine of them, plus Jochen.

'Has anyone ever flown in this stuff?'

Four hands flap up.

'By accident, when I was caught out,' Krueger says. A couple of others nod.

'I trained for all-weather flying when I was on bombers,' Schaefer says.

'Listen, I've been ordered up. You four may volunteer

to come. It's an invitation only, not an order. The rest of you are grounded.'

'We want to fly, sir.' Thomas, one of the grounded.

'No!'

Jochen walks off to get his kit. The four follow him. He turns. 'Are you all sure?'

'Of course,' Backhaus says.

He looks at Schaefer. 'You're the expert, Kurt. Any advice?'

'Keep your eyes on the artificial horizon. Don't trust your senses. You may feel you're banking or upside down or something. You won't be. Only the horizon knows. On the way up, spread out before you get into the cloud. On the way back down, when you get to a thousand metres, go slowly. Don't shoot out of the cloud at top speed.'

Jurg is by his Gustav in the rain. 'You're going up in this?'

'Orders.'

'What if I can't start her up?'

'No, Jurg. I'll just move on to another and then another until one does start.'

Bubi comes running up. 'What's going on? Are we going up?'

'Not you.'

'Why not?'

'I can't murder everyone, can I?'

In the cockpit he wipes his face and hands with the towel Jurg passes him. The leather of his US jacket glistens with water. He jiggles the stick around. All the controls move. They start engines. Darts of flame and bursts of smoke. He looks around. Whirring discs at the front of each Gustav.

'Off we go,' he says into his mask, 'and no chatter. Concentrate!'

They start to move across the grass. Rain runs down the windscreen but as his speed picks up, the wind blows it clear. They lift off in a wide spread and rise towards the cloud floor; nearly there and then a sudden disappearance of the world and he's into a claustrophobic grey mass. He drops his eyes at once to the artificial horizon and concentrates on keeping the two lines parallel. It takes an effort of will not to look out at the grey all around. He's heard enough stories of disorientation and the disaster that can result. He hopes they've all got their eyes glued on their instrument panels.

Time goes by. How long? He won't move his eyes to see his watch. It doesn't matter how long. But is that some light lifting the gloom in the cockpit? A quick glance up and he sees the grey now thinner, wispier, and immediately gone. Sunlight pours in through the canopy. He keeps climbing. The flat, level, grey cloud floor recedes beneath him. There are three Gustavs visible. He looks up at the blue above.

He's at five thousand now. Where are the Fortresses? Where are the Mustangs? They are so vulnerable like this, climbing at three hundred kilometres an hour with no information. There are still only three other Gustavs. He can't make out numbers.

'Check in, everyone.'

'Schaefer, here.'

'Backhaus.'

'Traube.'

'Anyone seen Krueger?'

A chorus of noes.

They climb still. Seven thousand. Glints in the sun, far to their left! Must be almost at the sea. Can they catch them?

'Heavy babies, nine o'clock, far away. Let's go!'

He turns after the Fortresses just as Backhaus calls, 'Mustangs, three o'clock!'

Jochen turns at once in time to see Backhaus's engine hit and start to burn. He fires at the Mustang as it passes in front of him, sees hits on the tail. Four more are coming down. They all point themselves at the Mustangs and Jochen fires when one appears in front of him. Tracers whip past him and he feels shuddering hits on the starboard wing, but he sees his own shells and bullets spark on the Ami's engine. Smoke starts from it. The Ami pulls up to pass above Jochen and receives several hits on that low slung radiator. Unconsciously, Jochen stores the radiator away in his mind as the best place to target. The Ami needs no more bullets. He won't get home.

Above the cloud floor the sky is clear. He looks at the wing to his right. Two holes that he can see. He pulls the nose up to follow the bombers.

'Anyone there?' he hears through the crackle.

'Murville here. Who's that?'

'Traube. Propeller shot away. I don't know where anyone is.'

'Waggle your wings, I might see a glint.' He looks all around. Nothing. 'Keep doing it.'

There!

'Got you.'

Traube's low down near the cloud floor. Two kilometres away to his right. Jochen turns towards him.

'Traube, jump now!'

'I can't, boss. The plane might land on a building. I'll have to fly it down.'

'Victor, victor. Drinks on me tonight.'

The glint has gone. Traube's in the clouds. Jochen turns to port again and the bombers. No glints there. He checks his watch. He's been up forty minutes. He's got no height to convert to speed if he chases them. If he does follow them, he'll overhaul them really slowly and catch them over the North Sea with ten minutes fuel left and still with Mustangs to fight. Time to go home.

In case anyone can hear him, he calls, 'This is Murville. Back to base, now.'

No reply. Radios unserviceable or everyone dead?

He banks to turn south to make sure he's over land when he emerges from the cloud and points the nose down gently, fixing his eye on the artificial horizon as he enters the clouds.

The altimeter unwinds. Two and a half thousand; two thousand; still the grey mass outside; one-and-a-half; one; still grey. He pulls the stick back a little to further slow his descent. At five hundred metres he's still in it. Lower, lower. He pops out at two hundred metres. The whole world feels grey, though he can see grass, a washy-green in the rainy mist, and trees, largely bare now. He has the cloud base as a horizon. He recognises nothing.

He checks his watch. Ten minutes before the red light. The land below isn't quite flat. Better to land now in a field than have to go back into the cloud to go over a hill. How's Traube getting on without an engine? If only it was the General in Traube's Gustav.

Over to his right a chimney appears, buildings around it, five hundred metres away? It rings a bell. A factory about fifteen kilometres from the field. He concentrates ahead again to avoid anything like that that might pop up, but there's a sudden flash in his peripheral vision. He swings the stick over to the right. Half the chimney's gone and there's a blazing mass at the foot of it. Jesus! Traube? No, he must be down by now. One of the others. Poor devil. That bastard General!

He sweeps his eyes across the land below and ahead of him for another landmark. A river! He passes over it. There should be – yes – there's the farm, cows in the fields, a man leading a horse drawing a laden cart. He puts the stick over to head west. Not far now.

The red fuel light is on as he joins the circuit and comes into the wind. He touches down, taxis over to the hard standing and swings the Gustav round to face the field. He's left tracks across the grass. Rain runs down the windshield. Jurg swings the hood up.

'Any luck, boss?'

'Probably a Mustang. Anybody back?' He can't see any of the Gustavs that took off.

'Not yet, boss.'

He squelches over to his office, slings his cap onto a chair, pulls off his flying jacket and throws it on the floor.

No one back! Schaefer's probably wrapped around that chimney; Backhaus probably burnt to death; Krueger didn't even get through the cloud, he probably spun in and buried himself in a field. Traube? Any of the above. He snatches up the phone to report the success of the General's orders but drops it before he speaks.

He sits behind his desk and puts his face in his hands. He's just led four of his guys to their deaths because the General's a typical bully; shouts at inferiors to intimidate them but is too scared to tell Fatty what's what. But then why didn't he just refuse to go? He could have insisted the weather was too bad. He was brave enough to limit the take off to four volunteers, but why did he even ask for volunteers? He should have gone by himself! The others would still be alive and ready for better flying weather tomorrow.

What does he do now? What would Winter do? What would he have done in the desert? Get the brandy out, toast the dead guys and write their names on the wall. The General can go stuff himself. He lights a cigarette. At least he kept Bubi and his *staffel* on the ground and all the other guys. There's a tap on the door.

'Come in.'

It's Scholz. 'Message from Leutnant Schaefer, sir. He's down at Jever. Got a Mustang. And Fähnrich Traube's just come in on the back of a motorbike. He got down wheels up in a field.'

Jochen beams. Two safe! 'No Krueger?'

'No, sir.'

'Leutnant Backhaus?'

'Nothing, sir.'

He grabs his cap and walks out, still smiling.

He's up at dawn. It's still raining but the cloud has lifted a little. A weather flight says it should clear by the afternoon. The airfield is very muddy.

Traube was soaked to the skin from his ride home on the back of a motorbike but elated at having done his duty, flown his Gustav down and survived. He kept his smile all evening as Jochen plied him with drink. Jochen's given him the day off. He has nothing to fly, anyway. Neither has Jochen but he'll take someone else's Gustav. They ended the night with songs. Jochen played the terrible piano in the mess for them until half past ten and then sent them all to bed. Finally alone, he played *The Golliwog's Cakewalk* and tried to recapture the feelings he'd had when he sat next to Lotte at his mother's church ladies at home the day they met and played it together. How enchanting she'd seemed; how taken he'd been with her concentration on the music; how she'd peered at it, pursed her lips.

But he knew the enchantment was all gone. It's a long time since he felt anything for her, since he even liked her. He was about to slam the lid last night, but he didn't. Piece of crap though it was, the piano had done nothing. He went to bed, laid an ashtray on his chest and smoked while he imagined Gerda in Sweden: having dinner around a civilised table, laughing at jokes, smiling at people with that little sideways smile of hers, smiling at blond Swedish giants whom she has beguiled and who will do anything for her. In return for an hour or two in bed?

He's drinking coffee when Scholz gives him the news about Krueger. He's the one who hit the chimney. He's dead, of course. How did he spend the hour between take off and chimney? Did he buzz around in the grey gloom all the time or did he zoom out into the sunshine above and battle with Mustangs and Fortresses all alone?

He carries out his duties, talks to the technical officers – engines, guns, radios, transport, flak. They all want something. An *Unteroffizier*, Fischer, follows him round and makes notes. They're ready for an alert but Jochen doesn't think they should fly. It's raining still and heavily overcast. It would be yesterday repeated.

Scholz finds him again. Backhaus is dead. He jumped from his burning Gustav and was found last night by a farmer, unconscious and horribly burnt all over. He died in hospital this morning – a mercy, really.

The mail arrives. He glances at the envelopes. His mother; Lotte. Lotte! And some writing he doesn't recognise. Not Gerda though. He pulls the envelope open. Hertha. Just a note. Hope you're well. She's finally got a few days off and is visiting her sister and nephew. It's lovely to be out of Berlin. The countryside is so beautiful, trees, grass, mud! But fresh air, too. She might try to transfer to the hospital there. They both sign, Hertha and Lilo, and Andreas, the baby, who leaves a smudge on the page. Hertha! She's great but... why did he go back that night? She said she wouldn't claim him, but he seems unable not to make his life more complicated.

A knock and Scholz comes in. 'A package, sir. Express from the Reichmarschal's office.'

Jochen undoes the package, opens the box – a fancy Berlin jeweller's name on it. Inside is a Knight's Cross with Oak Leaves, Swords and Diamonds, twin to the one that hangs at his neck, only, of course, according to Fatty, it isn't a twin, it's far superior because it has much better diamonds selected by Fatty himself and not the Führer. Who would know?

He pushes it from him. Is this how that grotesque man spends his time while his boys are burning to death and destroying chimneys with their 109s? He's momentarily overcome with melancholy. How much longer will they last? How many more dead before the end of it? He stares at the blank wall ahead of him. If he was at home in his room in Berlin, with Ilse's bedroom next door, empty since her murder, he'd weep.

He gathers himself. Go and see the guys. Light some cigarettes with Levine's zippo, that they all admire. Walk around the hangars, give everyone a cheery word. Visit the other *staffeln*, show his face, raise spirits, play the piano, pray there's no alert – it's still wet and overcast. He leaves his new priceless diamond-studded piece of junk in its box on the desk.

When he reaches the mess, they don't need him to raise their martial spirit. A report is in that yesterday, bombing through cloud over Wilhelmshaven, the Americans managed to hit a convent and a nearby hospital. Nuns and children dead. Guys are angry. They want the Amis to come again so that they can get at them. Jochen lets them talk. What can you expect when you can't see what you're trying to hit? And he can't believe, as some are shouting, that the Amis were targeting the convent and the hospital. It's just another hideous accident of war.

He goes back to his office and writes to the parents of the dead. No wives, no children, thank God. He starts with Krueger. Staunch comrade, fine pilot, a tragic loss to the unit, to the Luftwaffe and to Germany. How easily it flows from his pen, though it's all true. And he volunteered to fly. But he won't say that. It would be too awful to read that their boy needn't have been in the air at all, needn't have flown into that chimney. He's about to write that he died doing his duty but he stops. He can't. Krueger's death was the result of the General's refusal to face up to Fatty and Jochen's own foolish suggestion that he could volunteer. He should have gone up on his own. He will if the situation comes up again. But the letter sits there unfinished, unrounded off. But what can he say? Duty. It's what they'll want to hear. It'll be what they want to tell people. It might be a consolation. He writes it, ends with deepest sympathies, signs it and uses his *gruppe* commander's stamp at the foot of the page.

Backhaus's letter is the same. He doesn't mention that he burnt to death.

Still no alert. The gentle rain continues but the clouds seem to be lifting. He sends Berger off again for circuits and bumps below the cloud but in a Gustav this time. They have Backhaus's charred body and bits of Krueger's, so the adjutant has scheduled a funeral. Diesch dug his own grave in the corner of the field he smashed into, so he can't be included except as a name to be mentioned. If they aren't flying, everyone will attend.

Lunch is vile. Watery soup of no flavour and chewy meat supposed to be chicken. Black bread, very hard. Guys push it away. It's not good enough. These men are athletes; the work they do, the physical strain of flying; changes of pressure; changes of weight as gravity crushes them, fighting for their lives. He has an unsatisfactory discussion with the catering officer, who says he's scouring the countryside for something fresh every day. It's this stuff or tins. What's Fatty got for lunch? Steak or venison?

The afternoon wears on. The guys loaf around: write letters, read, play cards, a few kick a ball about. He'd like to join in but he's a Hauptman now and in command. He wanders over to the hangars, watches them work on the 109s, has a word with Jurg and then it's time for the funeral.

The chosen men line up. He inspects them. How Krause would laugh at the sight of him inspecting a parade and commenting on men's turn out! They march over to the graveyard on the edge of the airfield that holds those of the Luftwaffe killed around the area of Marx. Jonny Beck attends. Jochen reads a lesson. For everything there is a season. A time to live and a time to die. They sing a hymn. They lower the bodies. The guard of honour fires a salute. The rain ceases and the clouds separate.

The next day is a disaster. Much clearer skies and they take off with a big build up in Dora-Dora as usual. He gets a Lightning but no bombers and turns for home when the red fuel light has been on for some while. He barely makes it back. They lose seven Gustavs and four pilots. Schaefer gets a Fortress, their sole real success. Bubi has his right thumb shot off. Other units perform equally badly. The weather turns even colder, and snow falls in the evening. Everyone is despondent. They're not good enough. New guys who turn up are poorly trained and Gustavs are outclassed now; they can't evade the escort fighters to reach the bombers. After dinner they find some cognac, he plays the piano and they all sing. A signal comes in. All pilots to Achmer for 11am. A review by the Reichsmarschall. What can he want?

There's the sound of many engines high overhead and the never-ending crump of flak. It's dark and not their business at night, but he stands outside and watches the sweep of searchlights across the sky. The British bombers are passing on their way to somewhere else. Not Berlin, he hopes.

He can't go to bed. He'll only lie there and smoke and think about things he can do nothing about. He reads through combat reports, the unit war diary. He initials and signs pages when necessary, fills the tray on the right as he empties the one on the left. He's just gone outside to smoke in the fresh air when the airfield lights, such as they are, flash on. It must be a night fighter needing to land quickly. He hears a Jumo engine, only one; a Junkers 88 with a motor gone. The plane lands and taxis up to the hangars. He sees the red glow of the exhausts. How do they do it? Flying almost blind with a guy behind you staring at a green-glowing screen with a dot on it and calling directions in your ears until you get close enough to see something. He makes for the hangars. The

Prince, Heinrich zu Sayn-Wittgenstein, is shouting at his crewman, who's standing rigidly to attention.

'Yes, Major,' the man says eventually, and salutes as the Prince turns away.

Jochen leads the Prince to the mess and gives him cognac. His radar operator is an incompetent idiot. After tracking a bomber for ten minutes he lost the trace on the screen. And then he didn't spot the Lancaster whose rear gunner put their port engine out of action. How did he pass his training course? They have their subject, and they talk about the current state of the Luftwaffe: the lack of training, the poor equipment, the feeble leadership.

'He's probably got a new uniform to show off,' Heinrich says when Jochen tells him of Fatty's upcoming visit. 'He wants everyone to see it and applaud.'

'How's this all going to end?' Jochen says.

'It won't concern us if it goes on like this. We won't be here.'

Jochen glances round to see who's still in the mess but they're alone with their bottle.

'For everyone's sake, I hope the Yanks and the English get here before the Commies.'

'Amen to that,' Heinrich says. 'Hey, know what I did wrong when we were at the *Wolfschanze*? I should have known they'd take my Walther off me. I could have had another gun in my pocket. Something smaller, lighter.'

Jochen thinks at once of the Beretta .32 that he and Gerda killed Heinecke with. The one that he afterwards threw in the Baltic.

'You don't need anything big at close range like that,'

Heinrich says, 'two or three shots I'd have got off before they got me. We'd have been free of him.'

'You don't mind getting shot?'

'I've got no wife, no children. I'm expendable. You are, too.'

'Aren't you worried that I'll report you, though, talking like this?'

'You agree with me.'

'But it's treason, isn't it?'

'Oh, if you suddenly got a conscience, I'd deny it all. I could say, "On the contrary, it was that well-known anti-Nazi Jochen Murville who planned to do it. And I didn't say anything when he told me because I thought he was mad. All artists are and he's a renowned artist of the keyboard." They wouldn't argue with me. Everyone bows before my aristocratic mien. I'd say, "I'm a prince, you know." I'd probably get another private audience and then I could finish him off.'

They laugh. Jochen pours the cognac. 'You're the mad one.'

'It runs in the families of princes. It's the inbreeding.'

The Junkers needs a new engine, so Jochen finds a driver and sends Heinrich home in a *kübelwagen*. Heinrich allows his radar operator into the back seat but forbids him to speak. He and Jochen shake hands.

'Don't forget, we're both expendable,' Heinrich says.

Jochen sends his guys to Achmer in trucks. He doesn't want all his 109s parked in a mass with every other fighter from the area. A strafing run from a Mustang could cause havoc. He flies over to Achmer himself, though. By ten to eleven they're all lined up in ranks on the hardstanding with their feet in the snow. He's wearing his leather greatcoat. His Ami jacket would be inappropriate here. Goering's Oak Leaves with Swords and Diamonds is at his throat. He's scratched a mark on the reverse of the metal with a nail so he can tell his twins apart.

Ten minutes late, Fatty zooms up in a Mercedes limousine at the head of a column of twenty or so cars and half-tracks. Beck calls them to attention. Goering wears a comic opera uniform of a shamefully fancy design in grey, with gold all over his epaulettes and the peak of his cap, and scarlet boots of what looks like doeskin below tight breeches. He sweeps down the lines, looks into eyes, has a word here and there. A photographer follows him, taking pictures now and again. The light is poor and guys recoil a little, clearly surprised by the flash in their faces. When he gets to Jochen he reaches out to lift the Diamonds a little.

His nails are shiny. His usual varnish. There's a flash from the camera.

'You got it then.'

'Yes. Thank you, sir.'

'How are the legs?'

'Fine, sir.'

Jochen stares back at the face. Goering is flushed. No, it's rouge and surely that's lipstick, too. He catches a whiff of scent as the wind swirls around them.

'How many heavies have you got?'

'Eleven, sir.' Another flash.

Goering nods and goes on. Jochen follows Beck as they inspect the pilots in Jochen's *gruppe*.

When he's finished, Goering walks to the front to face them. His aides have set up a low podium and there's a microphone there, too. Is he going to sing? Jochen has to bite his cheek to prevent a smile at the thought. But it's not a song.

'That was fucking awful,' Goering begins. 'You can't even do a parade properly. In fact, I don't know what it is you can do properly because you certainly can't fight Americans, can you? You just let them fly all over Germany and kill nuns and children. Nuns! And kids! Have you got no pride?'

More than you, you perfumed slob!

'You're just a scared bunch of namby-pambies, keeping out of the big boys' way. Four B17s you got yesterday between you. Four! What's the fucking use of that? I should ground the lot of you and save the fuel. Don't you remember the RAF boys over London? Every day we thought we'd got the lot of them but the next day there they were again, snapping around, making life difficult for us.'

Oh, were you up there, too, Fatso?

'They were defending their country! Their motherland! Never frightened! Brave lads who flung themselves at us and died to save their homes! I'm ashamed to lead you.'

Lead?

'How can I explain your failure to the Führer?'

You'll think of something.

'If this happens again, heads will roll. Examples will be made of some.'

They should all volunteer. He will. He'll volunteer to be made an example of. Fatty won't have anyone left who can get a bomber.

'I'm going. Don't make me come back again.'

Goering steps off the podium and makes straight for his car without even the courtesy of a salute. His aides rush around dismantling podium and equipment.

Without really thinking and although it's not his position to do it, not being in command of the parade, and though he always tries to avoid it, but just to shame that mountain of lard a little, Jochen calls out, 'Heil Hitler!' and slings his arm up. Everyone follows suit. Goering is caught just about to climb into his car. He stops, glares at them all and raises his arm.

He's first back in his Gustav. Since there's no one there to disturb, he plays scales in the mess. It's a calming and nostalgic experience. He imagines himself long ago doing the same at the piano in their sitting room, his sister Ilse out at a friend's house after school to escape the noise, his stepfather still at work, his mother working on dinner in the kitchen, pleased with herself for having a son who can play so well, always urging him on, lapping up Herr Walter's praise of his playing, dreaming of a career for him on a concert stage.

He stops after half an hour. He should do scales every day and play two or three pieces as well. Use it or lose it. Playing songs for the guys to sing is no substitute for solid practice. He goes to the window. It's grey and bleak out. The weather guys say snow is on its way, a blizzard.

Perhaps they'll get a day or two off. The others will be back soon.

There'll just be time for lunch and, then, ready for the first alert. He goes to the gramophone and looks through the record pile for the Caruso he bought at the roadside in Berlin. He keeps the Beethoven he got at the same time in his room. An argument about Schnabel would be disagreeable in the mess. He doesn't want guys to have to take sides. He wants friends and comrades here not ideological opponents.

He winds the gramophone, puts the record on, starts it turning and then lowers the needle; instant crackle and hiss, not unlike the sound through the headphones in the cockpit of his Gustav but, oh, the message that comes through this interference is much more welcome, infinitely more sublime than 'Big build up in Dora-Dora'. There's that golden, pure voice. Just imagine it in a concert hall, minus the background noise! *Una Furtiva Lagrima*. Old Enrico! What a voice! Has anyone ever been better? He must be the Schnabel of tenors.

Jochen stares out at the airfield landscape under the grey sky: the distant parked Gustavs, the scurrying figures hunched against the cold. It's the right aria he's listening to. A furtive tear! Steeped in melancholy. The lightness yet the strength of the voice! And that wonderful melody! It would be right for a funeral. But not a service funeral, the guys need a lift after a death in the unit. At Ilse's funeral. It would have been appropriate. But could his mother have listened to it? Could he have? He's close to tears, listening to this and remembering his murdered twin; two years in the earth now.

4

Pathetique

Low clouds, snow showers, freezing winds, lousy weather. He wears his snug Yank jacket almost constantly, only takes it off to sleep and then lays it on top of his blanket.

Jonny Beck, the Nazi, their commander, exhorts them all to make Fatty's wish come true and knock down large numbers of bombers.

'How?' Jochen almost screams at him.

It's like their old days in the desert.

'We could bomb them again,' Jonny says.

A few months ago, someone tried it. A two hundred kilo bomb with a fifteen second fuse a thousand metres above a box of Fortresses. Too complicated, too chancy.

Frontal attacks. Frontal attacks. But they don't often get there to fire at the bombers, too busy avoiding Ami fighters. They chip away at the bombers but not enough go down to stop them coming; the same numbers are there the next day. There must be a conveyor belt from

America to England. Sauer goes down, Schulze, Jansen, Riedel, Albrecht, Weiss, a couple of other guys too, not in the *gruppe* long enough for him to learn their names until someone writes them on the wall with all the others. Bubi has a leather glove thing someone has made him that fits over the control column to help him fly with a missing thumb. They lose two more one day, three the next. The day after, they don't come. It's the 23rd of December.

'Day off. Christmas shopping,' Schaefer says. He's been to New York and he's their authority on things American.

He's up early alone on an engine test. No sun yet. His altitude makes it visible when he's at six thousand. He keeps climbing, feeling colder and colder. At eight thousand he spots a glint above him. He carries on climbing. Nine thousand. Ten thousand. He's level now. The glint has a shape. Two engines. Mosquito. It must be their daily meteorological flight. It would be nice to spoil their weather map but he's too far for a shot. Not even worth bothering. He climbs a little further and then the Gustav refuses. Is he gaining on the Mosquito? It looks a little bigger but then it puts its nose down and begins to get smaller. He chases in a dive but it pulls away. Just too damned fast. He goes home for breakfast. The engine's fine.

They lose two more. Jochen now has five more bombers and three Mustangs and a Lightning, but three times has landed with bullets in wings and fuselage. How long will he last? He's the best one there and he finds it hard. What can they expect the kids who turn up barely able to fly to achieve?

In the mirror while shaving he discovers grey hairs at each temple. He falls asleep on occasion at his desk as he looks through paperwork then lies awake most of the night, imagining warm Swedish sunshine and Gerda next to him on a bench, laughing.

Everyone's exhausted. He sends them off one by one for a few days rest at home or days and nights of debauchery as their fancies take them. Then Beck sends him off, too, for five days. Bubi will have the *gruppe*. It's mid-January. The train is slow and freezing cold. He longs for his Ami flying jacket, but he might get lynched in that.

There's more rubble in Berlin than when he was last here. People look dishevelled, dirty, downtrodden. Apart, that is, from the shiny staff officers who demand salutes and, with their women, seem to flit about above the new grim reality of wartime Berlin. He feels more and more melancholic as he trudges towards home. Where are all the girls from a year or two back that he'd exchange smiles with as they passed? How will his mother be managing?

There's been no time to write. His arrival will be a surprise.

Near home, he spots Frau Schreiber in a queue. He doesn't want to see her. Her son, his friend Bert, is assumed dead in a sunken U-boat and here Jochen is, alive and loaded with medals. But she turns and sees him. He starts a tentative smile, but she positively beams at him.

'Jochen!' she almost shouts. 'I've had a card from Bert. They picked him up. He's safe in England!' She laughs. 'He's working on a farm!'

It's a miracle. How many guys ever get out of a sinking U-boat? He runs up the stairs of their building and rings the bell but the footsteps he hears coming aren't his mother's.

The door swings wide and Lotte's astonished face stares at him for an instant before she throws herself at him, flings her arms around his neck and nearly knocks him over.

Later, Jochen walks Lotte home. They can't see each other's faces in the blackout.

'We go to the cellar,' she says, when Jochen asks where they shelter during a raid, and then, 'Are you going to come in?'

He can't bear the thought of kissing her mother, of having her sister call him brother, of shaking hands with her father, of losing to him at chess again, all in the glare of the lamplight in that once Jewish house. He says he must go back to see his mother. Lotte is immediately understanding. She's splendid, really. If only.

'Have you given Lotte a date?' his mother says as he throws his cap and greatcoat on the sofa and flops down next to them. He shakes his head.

'You're not the only fish in the sea. You'll lose her!'

He looks back at her. Silent. If only.

'You're waiting on that Jewish woman, aren't you?'

'Her name's Gerda.'

'I know that, but it doesn't matter what her name is, does it?'

He looks at her, still silent.

'I liked her,' she goes on, 'she seemed nice. But she's Jewish.'

'Mother!'

'Wait! That would always be a problem. That would be a problem anywhere in the world, let alone here, now. It would have been a problem when I was your age. Jews and Christians. We have our own beliefs. We don't marry each other. Just think what her family would say.'

'I think the Reich has solved that problem for her.'

His mother sighs. 'And she isn't here, is she?'

'No, thank God.'

'You can't have her, Jochen. She isn't here and never likely to be. But Lotte is. She's a lovely young woman. You make a beautiful couple.'

'So Goebbels told me.'

'Have you slept with her?'

'Mother!'

'If you have, it's your duty to marry her.'

He stares at the lamp in the corner.

'You're an officer and supposed to be a gentleman,' she says. 'You should follow your duty. It's what your father would have expected.'

The laugh has escaped before he can stop it. 'The man who left you?'

It's her turn to stare now. 'Never mind that.'

He picks up his cap and great coat. 'I'm going out.'

'You haven't eaten.'

'I'll get something somewhere.'

'You'll be lucky.'

Going down the stairs, he's immediately remorseful.

How could he have said that to her, 'The man who left you'. And she's only thinking of him, of course. What mother would want her son hanging about waiting for a Jewish woman who's hiding in another country and that he would have had great difficulty in marrying even at the best of times? He should go back. Apologise. But he doesn't want to start the conversation up again. He can apologise in the morning. Right now, he wants a drink. And he's hungry.

He finds a cab and asks for the Adlon Hotel, the only place he's certain will be able to feed him. The cab is a wood-burner; there's petrol for very few now. Up ahead, when he gets out, stands the Brandenburg Gate. The Kaiser used to pop down through it, he's heard, and take advantage of the Adlon's splendid heating to hold meetings with foreign dignitaries.

Up the marble steps and he's bowed in amongst the marble columns. He heads for the dining room. All the shiny staff officers in Berlin appear to have congregated here with their women, whose bare shoulders gleam in the lamplight, whose silk dresses shimmer and whose necklaces and earrings twinkle under the chandeliers. What are the chances of a table for one?

'But you must have a space somewhere,' he shouts to the Maître d' over the enormous hubbub in the room.

'If the *Hauptmann* perhaps knows someone in the room whose party he could join?'

Jochen glances around and is quite pleased to realise he knows none of these shiny-faced parasites.

'I'm afraid not.' He can always go to the club and see Otto. Perhaps Willi will be there and will cook him an omelette. He turns to go and almost walks into a Luftwaffe general with a moustache and a large cigar in his mouth, clearly just returning from the facilities. It's Galland.

'Murville! Trying to get dinner?'

Jochen nods.

Galland turns to the Maître d'. 'Bring another chair to my table.' Galland puts his arm round Jochen's shoulder and guides him across the room. 'Nice bauble there. Not as nice as mine, though, I expect.' Galland also wears the Diamonds at his throat. 'Fatty didn't like the diamonds Hitler got so he got me some better ones.'

Jochen laughs. 'Snap.'

Galland won't hear of an omelette, insists he has the venison. 'If any of your guys were here, they'd have it,' he says, when Jochen pleads guilt over the squalid rations his men are eating back at Marx. They talk about the failings of their Gustavs and the splendours of the Amis' Mustangs.

'Light me, will you?' Galland's companion asks him. He pulls out his zippo. She holds his hand to raise the flame to her cigarette.

'Forgive me, Baroness,' he says, 'talking shop like this.'

'Don't worry about it, darling, and call me Gisela. It's always the same when we meet any of his boys. Horsepower, rounds per minute, turning circles! Jabber, jabber, jabber. I'm used to staring into space. What he doesn't know is I'm composing my memoirs in my head. I'm going to dish the dirt on him. There, Dolfo! And I'll call you Adolf in them because you hate it.' She flicks back her blonde hair and smiles at Galland. She has green eyes and Jochen's immediately jealous that Galland has someone who'll make fun of him. Lotte would never do that now. Gerda would always be ready to.

He tells Galland about Goering's rant at them.

'He did the same in Sicily,' Galland says.

'He's not leading us, is he?'

'Where would he take us if he was?'

He starts off on Mustangs again. 'We'll all be dead before we know it.'

'Listen,' Galland says, and beckons him closer.

'Secrets time!' the Baroness says.

'Gisela! Keep it under your hat, Murville, but you just have to stick it out a bit longer and you'll have a jet.'

'Is it ready? The 262? How fast?'

'Nine hundred.'

'Nine hundred!'

'Shhh! Four thirty-millimetre cannon. And twenty-four rockets.'

'Rockets!'

'Don't forget to ask about the turning circle, darling.'

Jochen grins. 'Gisela! No turning in a baby like that, eh, General?'

'Never.'

'It's good then?'

'Wonderful. Like being pushed in the back by an angel.'

'How long before we get them? Weeks?'

'Months.'

Months!

'I'll be mincemeat by then.'

'Listen! I'll get you onto my staff. You'd be invaluable touring fighter stations and passing on your knowledge.'

'Please don't, sir. How could I look my guys in the eye as I tell them I'm leaving them in the lurch and going off to tour the country and dine at the Adlon?'

The Baroness offers to call a girlfriend to join them but for once he's thinking. He knows he has enough complications in his life, and he's played gooseberry long enough, too.

'Baroness,' he says, 'Gisela, it's been a pleasure.' As he stands to leave, he puts down some notes to cover his venison but Galland laughs and passes them back.

There's a raid. The alarm has sounded and there's the constant crump of the guns and the smell of smoke but no continuous engine roar of hundreds of incoming heavies, just the sound of a few isolated Merlins. Probably a dozen Mosquitos sent over to keep everyone awake.

At the club he sits in with Otto and the boys. Boys! Not one under fifty. Willi hasn't been in for some weeks and there's no news from Gerda. It's begun to snow. He makes his way home carefully. Apparently, there are large numbers of accidents in the blackout.

His mother has made biscuits and left some for him. The guilt he earlier felt at his behaviour towards her returns. The biscuits are tasty but not like pre-war. Bauer arrives home, late as usual, from the police department. He gets the brandy out, lowers his weight onto the sofa with a wheezy breath.

'What's up?' his stepfather says when Jochen's been silent for some time.

'I was nasty to Mother before I went out, but she's left me biscuits in case I couldn't get dinner.'

'I'm sure she worried unnecessarily You probably went to the Adlon.'

'Are you having me followed?'

'It's where I'd go to guarantee getting a meal. If I had the money.'

'I didn't pay.'

'A general did.'

'How did you know?'

'You make them look good sitting at their tables.'

'It was Galland. He doesn't need me to make him look good.'

'Your mother's worried about Lotte.'

'What do you think, Rolf?'

'I don't. If you were my son, I might. But look, they're in the same church community. If you ditch Lotte, there'll be talk. Anger probably. And you'll swan off. Sorry. That's inappropriate. You're not off to the Riviera. You'll go back to your unit and your mother'll be here seeing them regularly.'

'Lotte's a Nazi, Rolf. She believes it all. How can I live with her?'

'She's been brought up with it, Jochen. There are lots of people like that. Perfectly nice people. Apart from that.'

'I was brought up with it, too. I don't even like her now. How can she be a Christian and think like that?'

'Christians have always been vile to Jews.'

Jochen is silent. Bauer pours more brandy. 'Go to bed. Give your brain a rest.'

'If only I could.'

Bauer changes the subject.

'Heinecke's brother came to see me again.'

'Georg.'

'A chum, is he?'

Jochen laughs. 'He hasn't given up then.'

'It's probably something he comes back to when he has time. He is his brother.'

'Yes, mustn't forget he's officially just missing,' Jochen says. 'Keep him in the present tense. What did he say?'

'The same questions as before, really.'

'Didn't you tell him to fuck off, questioning a police administrator?'

It's Bauer's turn to laugh. 'Not a good idea to tell the Gestapo that. No, I answered him. Said the same things, we'd investigated his brother, told him what we'd found out.'

'Why?'

'It would have come out. He was asking all around. It's best to be as honest as you can be. You don't want to seem to be covering anything up. He asked about you. What you were doing the day his brother was last seen. I told you someone reported him in a shelter talking to a Luftwaffe officer who was accompanied by a woman, didn't I?'

'I remember you telling me.' Jochen thinks for a moment. 'So, I should be straightforward with him if I see him again?'

'Tell him as much as you can. Don't deny you were with a woman but decide who the woman was. Be clear why you can't disclose her identity. I told him I have little idea of your movements – a busy lad who gets about. A hero of the Reich, always in demand. And not my son, of course, so I can't demand things of you in the way your father might have.'

'My father would have told him to get lost.'

'I don't have the position and authority he had.'

'I'm just observing, Rolf. I'm very grateful to you for everything you've done.'

He goes to bed and lies there, thinking and smoking as usual. The Luftwaffe's on the road to annihilation. The jets won't appear in time to save it. And he'll be dead before they get there. And even if by a miracle he doesn't die, Georg Heinecke will catch him out in some lie or other. He'll never see Gerda again. What does it matter what he does? He can relieve his mother's suffering at least. Give her a respectable son. Give her an adored daughter-in-law.

Over breakfast he apologises to his mother for what he said about his father. His mother pats his hand. Hers is cold. Her hair is greyer. The war's making her older than her years. Later, he walks in the snow, his leather greatcoat buttoned up against the wind. Destroyed buildings are everywhere, piles of rubble, shabby people. If this goes on, there'll be nothing left of Berlin. How many have died? His mother's been lucky. She goes to the cellar in a raid but a direct hit would collapse the building on top of it. She should leave Berlin. She could join Hertha's mother in the country. A big house, many rooms. She and his mother are old friends. Wives of generals, their children; Hertha, Lilo, Jochen and poor Ilse at the same kindergarten and friends ever since. And the house is in Schleswig-Holstein, on the way to Denmark. Much nearer the British and the Amis when they arrive and, more importantly, further from the Ivans when they arrive. She wouldn't leave Rolf though.

He takes a cab to the Adlon again. He must be careful not to make it his regular haunt. He pays a fortune and has some real coffee. It's wonderful. Where do they get it? He feels guilty again over the crap his guys have to drink. He must stop the guilt. He's on leave. Only a few days. He can't help it that he can afford real coffee, black market coffee, he assumes. He should have brought his mother. She would love to be out with him and have people look at them. It would cost him nothing to indulge her pride. He calls at the desk on his way out and has a word about reservations.

He's outside the school at the time he knows Lotte usually finishes. He stamps around in the snow to keep warm. After a few minutes he gives in and climbs the steps to take refuge inside. He sits under the portrait of the Führer so that he doesn't have to look at it. The headmaster emerges from his office and Jochen tells him not to drag Lotte from her tasks. He's happy to wait. There's no wind in here but it's very little warmer than outside.

Eventually, he hears steps, and he stands. Lotte pushes through the door with her head turned as she calls goodbye to someone. Her head swings round and he sees her face, tired and expressionless for an instant before she realises it's him standing there. Her face beams and then becomes serious.

'Jochen! Have you come to tell me it's all over?'

Is she expecting that? Can he just do it? Like that? But he remembers his mother.

'What?' he says, after a moment.

'I always expect you to tell me you don't want to marry me after all. Every time I see you, I expect it.'

'Lotte. Let's get some tea.'

In the café, their usual one, the nearest to the school, they order tea but God knows what will arrive.

She seeks his eyes. Fixes them with hers. He stays silent till the waiter stops fussing around with crockery and leaves them.

'I've been so busy, Lotte. In the air every day, looking after the guys. It takes hold of you. It's difficult to think of anything else.'

She nods. She's so beautiful. Even looking tired. He must think about that. Her beauty. Keep in mind how he fell for her.

'Do you remember our duet that afternoon?'

She looks down, nods. 'Of course.'

'I often think of it.'

'Do you?'

'Yes.' Dive in. Say it now. 'I have three more days. We could be married on Saturday. If you want to.'

She fixes his eyes again. 'Do you want to?' she says.

Don't think. 'Yes. But Lotte, you must know I could be dead the next day.'

'I know. I've always known that.'

'You'd be my widow.'

'Yes.'

'You'd get my pension.'

'Don't talk like that!'

'Sorry. It's a joke among us.'

'Not for me.'

'No. Do you want to?'

'Do you love me?'

This is getting harder. He thinks for a moment. There's no way out.

'Of course.'

'Tell me.'

He breathes in. 'I love you, Lotte.'

'I won't be in a queue for you.'

'You told me that before.'

'It's still true.'

'You won't be in a queue,' he says.

'I want to marry you.' She swallows and he sees tears start to flow down her cheeks. She takes his hand across the table, raises it and kisses it. 'I love you, too, Jochen.'

He's taken home. A kiss from her mother. Her father and her sister are still at work. There's so much to organise so quickly! He tells them that this morning he booked a large table at the Adlon for an early dinner on Saturday. And a room. Just in case the answer was yes. They'll have to do all the formalities at the registry on the morning before the wedding.

What to wear? Lotte and her mother in a flurry. He says he'll leave but Lotte grabs his arm.

'Don't. Play something.'

He runs through scales for a few minutes then plays *The Entertainer* because he knows Lotte's mother enjoyed it ages back. Lotte gives a scowl at the Black American music, but he carries on. Her mother puts a large brandy on the piano and kisses his cheek. He looks through the music in the stool and finds the score of *The Pathethique*. It's the sonata Schnabel plays on the record he bought at the roadside in Berlin. Beethoven! The score is bookmarked at the second movement. He puts the music up. He's played it before but never learnt it. It's a slow movement though. He plays. The music is mesmeric and so melancholy. He's quickly lost in it. It goes on forever. But actually only a few minutes, of course. He imagines Herr Walter at his side turning the music for him, but the fingers that appear on the corner of the page are Lotte's. It's over. Time for the third movement. But he can't play any more of it. If he gets any deeper into it, he'll cease to function. He closes the lid.

'You shouldn't be flying, darling,' Lotte's mother says.

Then Lotte's sister comes in. She gives a little shriek at the news and kisses Jochen's cheek. Her father crushes his hand and puts his arm round Lotte.

'My little girl, young man!'

'Yes, sir,' Jochen says.

He refuses dinner. His mother will have something for him and anyway, he must give her the news and Lotte must still get up early for school.

His mother hugs him and kisses his cheek.

'My darling,' she says, 'I wish you and Lotte a long and happy life together.'

He has to go along with it. 'Thank you. We'll do our best.'

'If only...' Ilse was here, she doesn't say.

He tells her the arrangements.

'The Adlon! What am I going to wear? Frau Hofmann will look like a movie star as usual. I mustn't let you down.'

They eat the pie she's made from lots of winter vegetables. He's glad he had the venison last night. Then she's up and back and forth to her wardrobe and thinking aloud who she can borrow a hat from. After giving two or three opinions on dresses, coats, it gets too much for him. If only women wore uniforms.

He goes out into the blackness. No raid yet. Where have they gone tonight? Is Heinrich up there somewhere, cursing his radar operator?

The club isn't busy. He sends brandy to Otto and the guys, and sits at the bar and gazes into the mirror behind the barman. There's an empty stool next to him where Gerda once sat, years ago now. What's she doing as he sits here? In a similar place in Sweden? Sitting next to one of those Viking giants? Swinging her leg with that lovely ankle he wanted to circle with his hand the first time he met her. But it's silly to think of her like that. She's free. That's what he wanted. That's why he did it. He must be glad for her, whatever she's doing. He should think about his wedding, the happiest day of his life. But that thought brings him lower still. He gets out his cigarettes, looks down to light one with Levine's zippo.

'Nice lighter, Jochen.' Willi's face next to his in the mirror. He turns. They shake hands.

'A suit!'

'I know,' Willi says, 'how conventional I am tonight?'

They talk about the war, the state of Berlin, Willi's sons, still safe.

He sits in for Otto, circumspectly, because the manager is always anxious when Jochen is at the piano and he doesn't want to cause any trouble. Places are closed down sometimes now. It would only take an anonymous report. He plays *Schwarze Orchideen* and *Davon geht die Welt nicht unter*, the great Zarah Leander hit. People join in and sing.

Back at the bar Willi has a brandy for him. Jochen tells him about his imminent wedding.

'Aaah!'

'What?'

'Daughter of the eminent Dr Hofmann.'

'Yes. You were about to tell me about him, I think, when we came upon that bombed out building that morning.'

'He's very ambitious.'

'And?'

'Nothing else.'

Jochen knows there's something else. 'What else?'

'No. Really, Jochen.'

'I know there's something.'

'All right. He's a committed party member. Perhaps you know that but perhaps, from what I know of you, you might find that a difficult thing.'

'You're right, I do know, and it is difficult for me. But thank you for telling me.'

'I imagined you must know. He's quite enthusiastic, you could say. But you're not marrying him, are you?'

He plays once more, and Otto and the band congratulate him on his wedding. Willi claps him on the back as he leaves.

'I wish you a good life, Jochen.'

Willi is still watching him with a serious look on his face as Jochen turns at the door to look back.

At home, there's a telegram on the table. He tears it open.

Bubi in hospital. Serious. Beck.

Bubi. Serious. He'll die. That's what serious means. Another one gone. The one who saved his life in the desert! But why has Jonny sent a telegram? Jochen's on leave. He's getting married. Jonny doesn't know that, though.

He flops onto the sofa. Jonny wants him back, of course. Who's leading the *gruppe*? He runs through the guys in his head. It'll be Schaefer. He'll be good. If he lives. But he isn't good yet. Six weeks in Russia he had, got a couple of Ivans. Wounded. Back home. Six more weeks with Jochen. Trained on bombers first. Three or four Fortresses he's got and a Mustang or two. He's still learning, though. He shouldn't lead. Jonny knows that. He needs Jochen back. But he didn't say, *Come back!* How could he though? Not even Jonny could say that. Not to Jochen. But he told him the situation. It's clear he wants him back. Needs him back. But he's getting married. Lotte! His mother! He could go on Sunday morning. Be in the air twenty-four hours later. How many casualties in that time with Schaefer leading? They could be up four or five times in those two days. If he went now, he could be flying on Saturday morning. He might save a few lives. But Saturday's his wedding day.

5

Farewell

They take off soon after eleven o'clock. Concentrations in sector Dora-Dora. There's intermittent cloud and they enter and leave it several times as they climb. At ten thousand metres, clear of the clouds and under a deep blue sky, Jochen levels the *gruppe* off. Ice on the inside of the windscreen. The usual black puffs of flak in and around the distant but fast approaching tightly-formed boxes of bombers. There's the normal constant vibration through his body and the deep roar of the Daimler-Benz engine from in front of him that underlies the constant crackle and hiss from his earphones.

'Up again,' Jochen calls and pulls the stick back. Today they have to try to stop the Ami fighters from attacking the Focke Wulf 190s, which have been tasked with getting the bombers. A new tactic. Anything's worth trying. He looks around above them. Nothing. They must be there, though. But there are no glints visible in the sunshine.

'Indians!' Schaefer calls. Good eyes. 'Ten o'clock. One thousand below.'

They've managed to get above the Amis. A miracle.

'Anything over us anyone?' He can see nothing, and no one answers his call.

'Let's go.' He pushes the stick forwards and heads for the silver shapes glinting below. The Amis sail on. Are they blind? Perhaps they've come across a new unit. Never mind. Time to make hay.

Lightnings. He goes for the one on the right at the rear. Lagging a little. He fires as the short fuselage fills his sight. Sparkles all around the cockpit and the starboard wing, drifting out to the engine. The engine burns. The whole machine tips over to the right and begins to spin.

Then he's below the formation and pulling up beneath another. His fire hits the port engine. It burns and bits fly off. He's above the formation now and turning to the right, twisting his neck round towards his victim in time to see the pilot falling, tumbling through the air, and the remains of the Lightning pointing down at the ground getting rapidly smaller.

'Am I clear, Flo?' he calls to his wing-man.

'All clear, boss.'

The Lightnings' formation has broken up now, some diving, using their speed to escape. It's impossible to concentrate in this situation and hazardous, too, but he sees a Gustav behind a Lightning, hitting the Ami as it draws out of range, and another Gustav that zips across in front of him chased by a Lightning. He pulls the nose up and to the left. It feels right and he fires. Instant smoke from the port engine, then flames. The Lightning breaks off its chase. Jochen leaves the Ami. He won't get home.

'Jochen, break left!'

He does, instantly, and a Lightning curves past him followed by a Gustav. By the time he's completed his turn, the Lightning is minus its pilot, who's falling below the smoking machine that flies on ahead for a few seconds before turning on its back and spinning down.

'Thanks, Flo. Good shooting.'

He climbs, hoping to rendezvous with whoever's left. Back at ten thousand, he sees the bombers much, much closer, with some of the boxes looking less compact now. Three trails of smoke rise from much lower down. Small silver shapes are buzzing all around the Fortresses.

'Murville here at ten thousand. Who's up here?'

Flo calls in and five others.

'Check your fuel. If you've got enough, we're going down.'

Two call. Out of ammunition.

'Let's go!'

He puts the stick forwards and dives at seven hundred. Suddenly in front of him is a Fortress. Tracer whips past as he goes beneath the bomber. He pulls up and turns to starboard, and comes back from behind and beneath. The rear gunner is firing at him but the tracers don't fly close. He pulls the stick back and fires with the tail in his sight. Sparkles all over the enormous rudder. A huge 'D' painted on the silver metal. A large chunk flies off.

The rear gunner has stopped firing. Jochen drops his flaps to slow the Gustav and moves his aim to the port engines. He hits both and they begin to smoke. The ball turret gunner underneath the fuselage is firing at him. But Jochen is off to the side now. A much harder shot. He slides across to get at the starboard wing. The outer engine burns. Suddenly the bomb doors open and bombs fall. A quick glance shows open country below. Only cows in danger.

Get out, now. The huge plane swings round for home. Jochen pushes the stick forwards and to port to stay beneath and behind. He raises the flaps but closes the throttle a little to stay in formation with the Fortress. The smoke has ceased from the port engines but the propellers are feathered, the engines stopped. The starboard outer engine is still burning. The Ami is flying for home on one engine! How far does he think he'll get? He's still over Germany. Will he even reach Holland? Then he's got the North Sea. If they don't blow up before that. Jump! All of you, jump!

Jochen swings the stick over and pulls out to the right to watch.

'Are we clear, Flo?'

'All clear, boss.'

Sparkles come from the side gun and the mid-upper turret. They're still fighting! Tough boys. He weaves and dives and zooms to disturb the gunners' aim. The Fortress flies on towards home. Very slowly. Constantly losing height. Down to four thousand now. He wills them to jump. He'd like to buy them all a drink, the crazy bastards!

In his peripheral vision, a shape on his left darts across in front of him from above. A Gustav, aiming for the Fortress.

'Don't fire!' he shouts. But the final engine is hit and burns briefly before the whole machine explodes, leaving nothing but a cloud of black smoke and then falling, fluttering chunks of metal.

He gets back on the red fuel light and goes straight to the briefing room. He calls out above the hubbub.

'Who got a Fortress that blew up?' He looks from face to face. Heads shake. There are two missing. Schaefer. Not Schaefer gone! And Berger. But they got six Lightnings and one Fortress. Good but still completely useless.

Jochen is too disgusted about the Fortress to make any claim for it. Schaefer rings. He's down at Achmer. Berger is with him. Schaefer got a Lightning and shared a Fortress with Berger.

'It didn't blow up, did it?' Jochen says. But the answer is no.

He rings Jonny at *Geschwader* HQ. But he's down somewhere else. The guy on the phone knows nothing about a Fortress blowing up.

Refuelled, they go up again to meet the raid on its way back. They're jumped by Mustangs. Jochen hits one that makes off smoking. No one gets anything but they all get back.

He clears the papers waiting for him then thinks about what to write to Lotte and his mother. A glance at his watch. He'd have been married for two hours if he hadn't come back. They'd be eating at the Adlon. Drinking some of that excellent coffee. Dr Hofmann would be making a speech, perhaps. He would too. God knows what he would have said.

'I knew you'd be back,' Jonny said when Jochen arrived after sixteen hours on that freezing train, 'without my having to ask. Deep down you have a Prussian sense of duty.'

At least he didn't say National Socialist.

He tries to remember exactly what he said in his note to Lotte apart from telling her he'd been ordered back immediately because of Bubi's injuries. It's important to remember the lies correctly in order to avoid further complications. He knows he's behaved like a complete shit. He told her he loved her, arranged a wedding and then ran from it when the opportunity came up. Jochen never knew his father very well, but would he have done that? And what can he do now? He's stuck with his declaration of love and his proposal. He'll have to make some arrangement to go through with it. And as soon as possible. She's a perfectly nice girl. It's just that she's a Nazi. There are lots of nice people like that, according to Rolf.

It's dark by the time Jonny rings back.

'You did all right, I hear,' Jonny says. 'I knew we needed you back.'

'All right, but still useless. They'll keep coming in hordes. What happened to you? Out of fuel?'

'No. A bastard upper gunner shot my propeller off. But I got him. Blew up. Giant ball of smoke.'

'It was you! You bastard!'

'What are you talking about?'

'They had one engine left; I'd shot the others up. They were practically going backwards.'

'Why hadn't you finished them off then?'

'They'd jettisoned their bomb load. They must have

been just deciding to jump when you blew them up!'

'But why were you waiting?'

'To give them a chance to live, of course. They were brave guys. They'd still have a life but for you.'

'Brave? They're the enemy! What about the nuns and the kids the other week?'

'Accident. What could they see through those clouds?'

'Why didn't they take their bombs home, then?'

'When they could fly higher and faster without them?'

'You're too soft, Jochen!'

'You're a heartless Nazi fuck!'

'Mind your mouth! If I was there, I'd knock you down.'

'What's the punishment for attacking a fellow officer?'

'You tell me. You're the only one I know who's ever done it.'

Silence. Jochen sees the inside of the Fortress: the chipped green paint on the metal; cartridge cases sliding around on the floor; the gunners still at their posts, alert, swinging their weapons around; the rear gunner, who Jochen's probably wounded, bleeding over the metal deck, someone tending to him; the pilot staring ahead, deciding when to order his men to jump so that he can fly his aeroplane down to give the wounded guy a chance. The sweat. The stink of cordite, oil and fuel. The fear.

Jonny laughs. 'Since you think you'd already done all the work, I'll give you a half share in it.'

Jochen slams the phone down.

Anyone on an early morning engine test looks for the meteorological Mosquito. It gives the flight a bigger purpose. Jochen promises a bottle to whoever gets it. Schaefer fires one morning from a huge distance but the bottle remains unclaimed. The Amis emerge three or four times a week from sector Dora-Dora when the weather, as predicted by their Mosquito, is promising. Vapour trails at eight thousand metres, the silver dots that cause them just ahead, black spots of flak bursts that spread and disperse in the wind all around them. They strain to get above the bombers so they can dive on the fighters but, nevertheless, the Mustangs, Thunderbolts and Lightnings decimate them. Soon they won't exist. The mathematics is clear. The new guys, kids really, can barely fly. Jochen gets one here, one there; it's not like the desert. The old hands can take no time off. If they don't fly, the kids go up to be murdered.

A 190, newly arrived by road for the *staffel* across the field, bursts into flames immediately after taking off on a test flight. The pilot jumps, he's just high enough. The machine falls in some nearby marshland. They drag it out and find two flares stuffed between the cylinders of the radial engine. The Gestapo investigates. Sabotage in the factory, obviously, but they identify no culprit. A random couple of men are removed from the production line and shot, they hear.

'Traitors,' Jonny says.

'What can you expect?' Jochen tells him. 'Czechs, Poles, Jews, POWs forced to work in factories. Slave labour.'

'You know a lot about it.'

He does, of course. While they were on their escape trip, Gerda told him of the sabotage she saw in the factories she worked in.

'It's obvious,' is all he says to Jonny.

He's lying on his office floor one morning doing his stomach exercises when there's a knock at the door. He doesn't bother to get up. They all know he does this every day.

'Come in!'

It's Scholz.

'Package for you, sir.' Scholz puts a brown envelope on the desk and leaves.

Jochen finishes his leg raises before he investigates the envelope. It's addressed to Hauptmann Murville, and his *gruppe* and *Geschwader* numbers are on the front. It's clear it's a pistol when he picks it up. Not big. He gets a shock though when he slides the gun out. A Beretta .32. For an instant, he thinks Heinecke's brother has dredged the Baltic and sent the murder weapon to him as an accusation, but there's a short note inside.

Over to you, Jochen.

Good shooting,

Heinrich.

He understands. Zu Sayn-Wittgenstein is dead. He picks up the phone and asks to be put through to Heinrich's unit.

Killed. Two nights ago. And his crew. They don't know what happened. A Lancaster gunner perhaps. The package was in his effects to be sent on to Jochen. Heinrich believed Jochen would take on the task of removing Hitler and has left him the gun he had ready. Jochen should have pooh-poohed the idea more effectively.

A letter arrives from Bubi in a child's careful hand. Two pages. He's dictated it to his sister, he says. The headaches are less and less bad. He feels improvement every day. The leg is getting stronger; he'll be hopping around with a crutch soon. He practises bending his knee every day and there's more and more movement. He can't wait to get back. A Luftwaffe doctor, a major, hung his knight's cross around his neck as he sat to attention in bed. It was very amusing. They're having a party in the ward tomorrow for his birthday. A nurse is baking a cake. God knows what she'll find to put in it. Greetings to whoever's left that he knows.

Birthday. Twenty-one? It must be. He was nineteen when he stopped Jochen being dragged across that rocky stretch of desert. Twenty-one!

He looks at the second page. Adult writing but not Bubi's.

Forgive my adding something, Hauptmann. You won't know from his letter but Martin is quite dreadfully injured. His face is burnt and gives him terrible pain, his leg is bad, they feared they would have to amputate it. He was unconscious for nearly two weeks and has constant headaches from his fractured skull. Yet he talks of getting back to you all soon. Please forbid him to. He's so headstrong and we're all so worried that he'll just take it into his head to get up and go back before he's ready. He says he's letting you down lying in bed. He's devoted to you and talks about you constantly. He'll be much more use to you later when he's fit and properly well.

It's from Frau Schuster, Bubi's mother.

He smooths the page and reads it again. He was warm after his exercise but now the chill in the office has come over him. He pulls on his Ami flying jacket, lights a cigarette with his Ami zippo. If only there was an Ami Mustang waiting outside for him. He picks up the phone and tells Scholz to get Bubi's hospital on the line and then asks him for his family's address. He waits on the line for Bubi's doctor to be found and then gets the true gen on Bubi's condition. Of course, it's his mother's version. A year, if he's lucky, before he flies again? Good, it'll be all over by then.

He writes to Bubi's mother. He tells her he owes his life to her son and how long he took to recover from his own injuries, that it's likely to be as long for Bubi and that he'll write and tell him to prepare himself for the long haul. He writes to Bubi as promised, saying he spoke to the doc and tells him to get properly well and sends his birthday greetings.

A call comes in. Concentrations in Dora-Dora. He drops the letters in the out tray as he leaves.

In the dark, they hear engines going over for hour after hour, but no bombs fall. They see search lights thin as needles in the far distance to the south-east and the very faint crump, crump of flak. There are hundreds and hundreds of them. Those airfields in England must be choc-a-bloc; Lancasters parked out wing tip to wing tip before they all leave for Germany.

They agree from the noise that the direction seems to be Berlin. They drift off to turn in and anyone from the capital is left alone with his thoughts. His mother will be sitting in the cellar of their building with her knitting, surrounded by her neighbours, probably with just a couple of candles giving light. Couldn't she leave the city? A million have, apparently. Bauer could survive without her; he was a soldier once. And he wouldn't have her to worry about. Lotte's in a cellar, too. She could go, as well. He doesn't love her but he thinks he did once; he doesn't want to see her dead. Lots of children have gone. They need their teachers, don't they?

In the morning, there's no chance a private call will be put through to Berlin so he pretends it's official business. After a wait of an hour and a half, he's finally connected to his stepfather at Police HQ.

'She's safe,' Bauer says. 'In the cellar all night. I didn't get home. She was quite calm this morning when I did. Our building wasn't hit but it's a miracle it wasn't. God, the mess! Buildings down all over. Smoke and dust everywhere. We need the army here to dig everybody out but there's no chance of that, is there? What we've got is the Hitler Youth. I can't talk long, we're up to our eyes in it. It's chaos. God knows where people are going to sleep. There was a wind, and everything went up like a bonfire. They're still trying to put it out. I hope to God they don't come back tonight. Sorry, Jochen, but I've got to go. On top of everything, we seem to have a guy going round killing women in the blackout. There was another one last night during the raid. After all these years, I'm still amazed how weird people are.'

'Wait, Rolf. One second. I know you can't go, but would mother leave? Go somewhere? Out of Berlin?'

'I don't know. But it's a terrific idea. I wish she would. I could relax a little with just me to worry about. I'd have to talk her into it, though. Be persuasive. You know your mother. I expect she'd feel guilty leaving me. But where? Not east.'

'God, no! She's better off facing bombs than the Ivans when they get here.'

'You think they will? Don't answer that. Switchboards! I've got to go.'

There's no sign of the Amis. He grabs some paper and starts to write. *Dear Hertha...* But then he has a better idea. If he writes, it'll be days there and days back. He buzzes Scholz.

'What's the nearest field to Neunerstadt?'

Scholz buzzes back a few minutes later. Jochen's just put the phone down when the Amis are announced in Dora-Dora. They kit up and take off. Twenty-three of them today from the three *staffeln*. Ice inside the windscreen; crackle and hiss through the earphones; Mustangs diving from above but called out by Schaefer in time for them all to make a climbing turn into them. A snap shot into a radiator that will leave the Ami to come down somewhere long before home and then a spiral climb to get above them before the Mustang chasing a Gustav fills his sight. He hits the cockpit and engine, and it goes down in a smoking dive that becomes a vertical fall from eight thousand metres. The Fortresses fly on south-east. Not Berlin again! Distant black dots of flak mark their progress.

As he's landing and sees his airfield below him, flying over ground crew working on Gustavs parked haphazardly on the hard standings in front of hangars, he has a dreadful vision of the future.

He calls *staffel* commanders and crew chiefs together and tells them to clear undergrowth and get all their machines under cover amongst the trees that surround the field.

Jochen's goes in first. Not pulling rank. His is the most valuable machine because he is the most valuable pilot. He taxis out of the trees at very first light, takes off and flies up into the dawn on a dual-purpose flight. Success in the first purpose will assuage his guilt about the other. At ten thousand the air is clear and very cold. The ice is on the windscreen as usual. The cold penetrates his Ami jacket, his tunic, his jumper, his shirt, his silk underwear. The Gustav struggles up to nearly eleven thousand but doesn't respond very well up here.

He stares west. Nothing. Aren't they coming today? Then he sees a far distant glint. He flies to the left, hoping to get behind and cut off its escape route. The Mosquito comes straight on. He'll be invisible behind. He swings to left and right to check behind himself; don't forget basics.

The Mosquito is a little above Jochen, but he can't coax his Gustav any higher. At two hundred metres below and behind it fills his sight and he fires. The port engine bursts into flames. Get out. He fires at once at the starboard engine. Smoke starts from it.

Get out! They won't have long now in a wooden aeroplane. The flames from the port engine stop and the smoke from the starboard, too. Fire extinguishers. Neither propeller is turning.

The nose of the Mosquito goes down. Is he going to glide down? Or is it just too high to jump? Jochen keeps them company and checks around that no other Gustav is sidling up to blow the Mosquito apart. At six thousand he spots a flame starting again in the port engine.

Jump! Jump! Have they seen it? They must have an instrument to tell them. The plane levels off and a hatch in the side flies off. A shape tumbles out. Part of the canopy goes and a man struggles up and finally out. They fall and fall but eventually their parachutes stream and deploy and Jochen feels like singing. As they float down, he sees the Mosquito plummeting. It's become almost invisible when there's a flash in a field far below.

He leaves the falling men and turns away towards his next destination. He calls in and announces, 'Mosquito down,' and gives an approximate map reference for the wreck and its crew.

Scholz has done some work on the phone for him so when Jochen lands he asks immediately for Hauptmann Becker. The Diamonds at his throat have their usual effect and a *leutnant* is honoured to take him to Becker, who provides him with a *kübelwagen* and a driver who knows the area. Jochen gives the driver a cigarette and says he's going to sleep. He puts the collar of his Ami jacket up against the draught between the window and the canvas hood and closes his eyes. It's twenty-five minutes later when the driver nudges him and he wakes to the sound of their tyres on gravel. There are leafless apple trees on either side and a gentle curve to the drive. Halfway up as they pass a huge and grand oak, a substantial brick house appears, square with a mansard roof. Would there be a room for his mother up there beneath the grey tiles?

It's only when he's about to pull the bell that he realises it's not even eight o'clock. It can't be polite to call so early. But what can he do? There's a war on. He waits and waits and has his hand on the bell to ring again when the door swings open. Hertha in slacks and a thick jumper and her hair tied up in a scarf. And her mouth wide open. Finally, she smiles.

'You know how to make an entrance, don't you?' she says.

He leans forwards to kiss her cheek, but she doesn't turn her head and so his kiss is to her lips.

'I landed nearby. I thought I'd say hallo. Can I come in?'

'Of course, but wait here. I'll be straight back. There'll be three heart attacks if I take you into the kitchen without warning.'

She leaves the door open a crack. He hears a distant shriek and a cry of 'Jochen?' that must be from Lilo, then scurrying feet. Hertha returns and leads him through a panelled reception hall and on into a tiled and cosily warm kitchen; a large table with cups and a breakfast cake on it and a colourfully-tiled stove in the corner.

'I'm the only one dressed in any way decently and that's only because I was on my way to collect the eggs and muck out the chickens before I start my shift at the local hospital.'

'You're as beautiful as ever.'

'Still the silver tongue. How's Lotte? Married yet? I haven't had an invitation.'

He tells her about the on then off wedding. She shakes her head at him.

'Have you come to see me, then? You didn't write back.'

He feels like a shit again. He tells all. Her face falls a little, but she quickly bucks up.

'I'll have to talk to Lilo. Margarethe is *her* mother-in-law. Mother and I are just guests. I'll see her now.'

She leaves him with acorn coffee and hot milk. He's raising a large piece of cake to his mouth when the door opens. He lowers the cake and stands.

'Frau Deichmann.'

'Aunt Vicky, Jochen, please. How lovely to see you!'

They kiss cheeks. They talk about Berlin, his mother, his dead father and then the door opens. A large woman with a wide smile, a mid-calf navy blue skirt, a blue jumper and pearls.

'So, you're the famous Jochen Murville I hear about all the time.' It's Lilo's mother-in-law. 'Call me Margarethe. And give me your Berlin address. Lilo has told me everything. I will write to your mother at once and you can take the letter back with you. It will be lovely to have her here. Three old ladies to keep these chits of girls in order.'

Last in, Lilo, clutching her baby to her, bright and smiling as ever but with dark-ringed eyes, exhausted from the baby probably and from worry over her husband captured at Stalingrad. Or dead. The baby, Andreas, is smiley and bonny and takes an instant liking to the diamonds. Jochen holds him and the baby's hands are all over them. He cries when Jochen hands him back.

At Jochen's request, Hertha takes cake and coffee out to his driver.

'He seemed surprised,' she says.

'Always look after the men. The old man told me that.'

The time is getting on. He has to go. He must be there if the Amis come.

'Oh, play us something first, Jochen,' Lilo says, 'I haven't heard you for so long.'

He protests but Lilo leads him to the piano. He riffles through their music, finds something he's played before but doesn't know. He flicks his hands free from his cuffs and begins. He doesn't look up and doesn't see them gazing at him as he concentrates. It's a wonderful piece. Well, it's Chopin, so of course it is. He lifts his fingers after the last notes have died.

'Beautiful, beautiful,' Margarethe says. She's standing at the door with the letter in her hand.

'Yes,' Hertha says. 'What is it?'

'A waltz by Chopin called *Farewell*.'

'*Farewell*! I might have known. Chopin. Old misery guts! It's my birthday on Saturday.'

'Seventeen?' Jochen says. 'Happy birthday from Chopin.' He plays the internationally known tune in the style of Chopin. They all laugh and applaud. 'And from Beethoven.' He plays it loud and thunderously. More laughter. 'Finally, from Scott Joplin.' He plays a ragtime version, stops, lowers the lid, stands, bows and grabs his cap.

Hertha sees him out. In the hall he kisses her.

'Thank you so much, Hertha. You're wonderful. And much too good for me.'

She smiles, just. 'I am, aren't I?'

He's back by twelve. But no Amis. He sends Margarethe's letter of invitation off in the official bag inside another envelope addressed to Rolf Bauer at Police HQ Berlin. They lie around, sleep, play cards. In mid-afternoon, Jochen's Mosquito crew turn up, pilot and navigator, delivered by *kübelwagen* from the fields they landed in. They give them tea. Foul tea and revolting sandwiches. Jochen is embarrassed. The pilot is limping. Peter Jessop, a flight lieutenant, a DFC. From Surbiton, in London. Jochen writes down the address. The navigator is Canadian, from Ontario, another flight lieutenant, no medals. Charlie Price. He gets his address, too. He leaves them their watches. He can't take everyone's into safe keeping. Perhaps they'll get lucky and no one will steal them. He packs them off for interrogation with a big grin.

'Tell them nothing,' he says. 'And be careful, they'll try to trick you.'

Later, they hear it confirmed that the Ivans have raised the siege of Leningrad. Many Germans captured, the rest in retreat. His buoyant mood pops. The guys settle into twos and threes to talk. How can he lift them? But perhaps they need to talk first. The Reich is clearly in deep shit. They need to work that out for themselves. He can't just jolly them out of it. In fact, he shouldn't. It's not a dead comrade to remember and toast, it's mad dreams going up in smoke.

He's moving piles of paper from one side of his desk to the other when Scholz comes in. There's a letter with a Berlin postmark. He doesn't know the writing but when he turns the letter over, he sees the writer's name and address.

Willi! He opens it at once and reads it. Then he reads it again. He can't believe it. Then he does believe it and he's deeply shocked. Then he's disgusted, revolted. Then angry. In fact, furious. Dr Hofmann! That smiling paterfamilias with the protective arm around Lotte. 'My little girl, young man!'

6

J'attendrai

The contents of Willi's letter reverberate in his mind. They lie there below everything and seep up into all his daily concerns. He needs to see Lotte's father, question him. But he's in Berlin. Jochen can't just up and go.

The Amis don't come. He does paperwork. Their Gustavs are dispersed in the woods now, invisible from the air. How long will it take the Amis to work out where they are though? An airfield empty of aeroplanes every time the Mustangs fly over? They must wonder if they can all be off fighting all the time. If he were them, he'd bomb the woods. Just to be sure. A few incendiaries would do the trick.

Schaefer's got hold of a shotgun and goes out towards dusk after the rabbits that hop about at the far end of the field. Their dinners have improved. Jochen insists the rabbits are shared around among the men too and not hogged by the pilots. A new guy arrives with a few records. A couple of

Zarah Leanders, always popular, and Rina Ketty. *J'attendrai*. One or two protest. It's in French. Of course, it is, Jochen says, Ketty's French. He loves the tune and catches himself humming and whistling it. It's so evocative. 'I will wait.' Just imagine it. The warmth of Gerda in his arms. Nothing to do but dance with her. All day, all night.

The Amis come. A better day. Two Thunderbolts, two Fortesses, one loss. A new guy, Koch. The one who brought the records. Poor devil. Jochen has nothing to say to his family apart from he was a nice guy. He manages to expand that when he writes. Four victories to one loss. The ratio is acceptable, but the numbers are pathetic, piffling. They won't stop them coming like this.

Everyone has accepted the end of the fighting at Leningrad. For the first time, Jochen hears someone say that the Reich should make peace with the allies so that together they can destroy the Commies, who are the enemies of all mankind. Jochen plays and they sing after dinner, including *J'attendrai*, in French, which seems to have ceased to be an unpatriotic thing to do.

Lotte writes. She longs for him to come back so that they can marry. She understands entirely that he had to go that day. He is an officer, a leader. It was his duty. His note and afterwards his letter made it all so clear. It helped her get over her disappointment. What matters is that he told her he loved her. That makes everything bearable. But she longs to see him. For a moment he feels awful but immediately remembers that she has a vile inhuman monster for a father, so what does that make her? He throws the letter aside. He may never answer it.

The next morning there's a letter from Otto; his name's on the back. Jochen's never been so popular. Otto's never written before. It feels thick. God! What's happened? He pulls it open and there's another envelope inside. Is it…?

Jochen Murville, Luftwaffe.

No one else would write that. He turns it over. It is her! Her address is on the back! He knows where she is now! He can find her later! Afterwards. Sometime. One day. As she said. 'One day, Jochen.' He slides the paper knife along the fold of the envelope. Of course, there'll be no afterwards, there'll be no 'one day'. He'll be dead.

He pulls the letter out. There's a photo there. He holds it only for an instant before dropping both photo and letter onto the desk. She gazes up at him from the desktop as beautiful as ever, smiling fit to bust, while the baby she holds in her arms with its face close to hers stares out with lovely and slightly vulnerable eyes.

He's shocked and can't think. Who's baby? One of those Swedish giants? So much for 'one day'! The phone rings. A reflex extends his arm.

'Concentrations in sector Dora-Dora, sir.'

He turns from the desk and grabs his Ami jacket on his way out, leaving Gerda and her baby where they lie.

They're directed to climb out towards the coast. They're at eight thousand metres and have just spotted the distant Yank boxes when they're bounced. Only one guy sees them.

A voice shouts, 'Break!'

No name attached to the cry, no direction. Without thinking, Jochen pulls the stick over to the left and further back. They'll expect a dive to escape and won't be able to follow immediately. As he rises and turns, he sees someone jump from a blazing Gustav, no number discernible. He sees a Thunderbolt in front of him, coming down, part of a second element diving on them. He fires but the Ami has left his sights. There are more coming down; black cross shapes that swell into aeroplanes. Too many to count. They took off with fourteen in the *gruppe*. There must be three or four times as many Thunderbolts attacking them. They'll be slaughtered. Is anyone there? He calls his wingman but there's no answer.

Now what? Get away or fight? He's heading towards the sea. Waves are breaking white on the shore far below. He's still climbing but he sees a Thunderbolt five hundred metres below behind a Gustav that's weaving for all it's worth. As he puts the nose down and pulls full boost, he glances around through the canopy as well as he can between the glazing bars. Nothing near him. The Thunderbolt grows and fills the sight. As Jochen fires and sees sparks around the wing root, the Ami breaks to the right, away from the Gustav he's chasing. Jochen breaks left. The Ami's been warned on the radio and whoever's behind Jochen may expect him to follow the Thunderbolt.

As he turns, he sees a Thunderbolt behind a Gustav behind a Thunderbolt. He puts his nose down to the right and then left to straighten up behind the Thunderbolt. It fills his sights. He fires. The Gustav loses speed from the recoil as he does so. He sees sparks all over the tail, then the cockpit, and the Ami goes into a spin towards the grey sea below.

He banks and the sea is to his left now, the sky to his right. But too late. The starboard wing shakes as rounds hit it. He cuts the throttle and pulls a tighter turn. A Thunderbolt flashes past and is gone. He's at five thousand now and way out to sea. Too far out. He straightens up, pulls full boost and puts his nose down towards the coast and the line of white breakers far ahead.

Three tremendous bangs shake the Gustav and the engine bursts into flame in front of him. He drops the flaps and fires his guns. The straps dig deep into his shoulders as the flaps and the recoil from the guns decelerate the Gustav instantly. A Thunderbolt shoots past him and flies into his sights. He fires and keeps his thumb down. The Ami takes hits all over; the fuselage, the wings, the cockpit, the engine, which starts to burn. Jochen's cockpit is full of smoke, and flames are starting around his feet. He's over the sea but he's got to go. Leads out of the helmet, straps undone and a climb into the slipstream over the side of the cockpit this time.

He dives forwards and down to avoid the tail that did him so much damage in the desert. When he sees the Gustav far away from him and falling to the sea nose first, he pulls the cord. Nothing for a moment and then a tremendous jerk sets him right way up and he's floating over that bleak sludge-coloured sea that, in fact, he's falling towards quite rapidly.

How cold? How long has he got? He was in the English Channel for an hour but that was in September when the water had had a summer to warm up. Now it's just March and the Baltic has had a winter to cool down. He should have married Lotte, his pension would come through in a couple of weeks and she'd be a highly eligible and desirable widow.

He'll have minutes, he decides, once he hits the water. He looks all around below and sees another parachute floating on the water three or four hundred metres away. The Yank? In the other direction he sees… is that another parachute? No! A sail! A sail? How far? Five or six hundred metres? How long to sail that far? That's supposing they've looked up and aren't concentrating on their nets. But surely, they'll have heard the engines, the shooting?

The sea is rising rapidly towards him. The drill is to press the quick release and slide out of the parachute just before he hits the water. Some hopes. The sea is freezing as he plunges in and the shock of it snatches his breath from him as he goes under. Still under, he manages the quick release. The cold is already eating into him. He struggles out of the straps and as his life jacket pulls him to the surface, he makes sure he's entirely clear of the straps and the parachute that could drown him if a wave tumbled it under and down. He splutters and gasps as he spits out most of the water he's swallowed.

'Fuck! Fuck! Fuck!' he can eventually shout out against the cold. Icy water slops over his head every few seconds. He glances at his watch.

The life jacket keeps him on his back, looking at the sky, an uneven sunless grey. When he rises on the crest of a wave, he can see the boat. When he's in a trough, it disappears and the grey water looms high all around him, lowering and threatening, as if anticipating and planning how best to kill him. Freeze him or drown him? Each time it reappears, the boat has its prow towards him, sailing, it must be, because there's no longer fuel for an engine. Surely, they've seen him? Two guys probably, like Uwe and Herbert, who took Gerda to Sweden. She's right to have abandoned hope of him. Right to have found a fine blond Swedish guy to make babies with. What else was she to do over there all by herself? He's recovered from his shock at the picture. Now he's about to die, he's happy for her. It was the surprise of seeing it without warning that made him so ungenerous. And he couldn't do anything for her now anyway. He can't do anything for anyone, not even himself. If that boat misses him, he'll die here. Be washed up somewhere eventually; a corpse on a beach. Him and that other guy over there, who must be bobbing up and down just like Jochen. His mother will hear at last, ending that horrible missing in action period; weeks, months. He'll be unrecognisable. Bloated, face eaten by fish; a horror for whoever rolls him over on the sand. They'll have his ID tags, though. They'll know him.

He can't feel his feet, his legs, any part of him really, now. He imagines himself sitting on a bench in the sun with Gerda and her guy. An old friend visiting. Smiling and laughing, tickling the baby he holds as it plays with the diamonds at his throat. How lovely to fall asleep in the sun after lunch on that bench, so warm, so comfortable. He closes his eyes for a moment. The sun is so warm on his face, on his body.

Jesus! He jerks awake. Don't sleep! He twists his wrist to see his watch but it's under his cuff and he can't remember when he went in, anyway. It must be many minutes by now. On the next crest the boat definitely looks closer. Stay awake! Stay alive! Gerda said that to him a couple of times. He wants to see her again whatever her situation. He must give himself the chance. Stay awake. How would he do that normally? Dash cold water on his face. He'd laugh if he wasn't dying.

Sing!

All that comes to mind is *J'attendrai*. Absurd. But he sings it. In French. Though, after three lines, the words disappear from his mind. Only the tune remains, which he 'la-las' at the top of his voice.

Up on the crest. Down in the trough.

As loud as he can.

Something takes an arm, then the other. He looks up. A boy leaning over the side of the boat, holding him. Then another figure. Ancient looking. His grandfather? They drag him over the side, scrape him on the top and dump him on the deck. Water flows out of him and into the gunwales.

'Where are you hurt?' the old man says.

'Not hurt,' Jochen manages to say.

'What was that terrible noise you were making, then?'

'Singing.'

The old man laughs. 'You won't win any competitions.'

They drag him below. He continues to shed water.

'Another man,' he says.

'We saw him. We'll get him.'

The boy goes above to steer and handle the sail and the old man helps Jochen out of his clothes, leaves them in a pile and gives Jochen two blankets. He passes a small flask. Jochen takes a swig. Brandy. He coughs and hands it back. It's the boat's first aid kit. The other guy will need some. He sits and shivers. He's a block of ice.

He listens to the two on deck shout nautical instructions to each other. He understands barely a word. It's their lingo. They wouldn't understand his radio speech in the air. He moves his extremities.

They seem to be coming back to life. He wiggles his toes; frozen but they move. His fingers, too, white. He puts them in his mouth. Like sucking an ice cube, a salty one. They reached him just in time. Two more minutes and his singing would have slurred to a stop. He'd have fallen asleep. He rubs his hair with one of the blankets, then his arms and chest. The blood begins to move. The rubbed areas of skin tingle, then, 'Aaarh!' Pain like knife blades courses through him and goes on. Slowly, very slowly, the pain subsides.

The boat rises and falls, much as he did in the waves; the same crests and troughs. This must be what causes the famous sea sickness.

He stands, bending under the low deck. He stamps his feet in an attempt to get feeling back into them. The below decks area is tiny. He and the other guy will fill it.

Where will his saviours go?

The boat stops moving forwards, begins to wallow, rising and falling. Have they reached him? There's a lot of shouting, gasps and grunting. He pokes his head out of the door. The guy's parachute is a bundle on the deck, the shrouds trail back into the sea. The two hang over the side, the boat heeling as they lean, clutching the guy, he assumes.

'We'll have to let him go,' the old man shouts to the boy.

'No!' Jochen shouts in turn.

'He's dead,' the old man calls over his shoulder.

'Doesn't matter!' Jochen calls.

They struggle on and the body in an Ami flight jacket slides over the rail. They fall back and the body rolls on top of them.

'Shot in the groin,' the old man calls, 'must have bled out in the sea.'

The boy is white-faced and staring. He's what, fourteen? His grandfather sends him off to steer. Jochen watches him go. After a few steps the boy stops and vomits over the side before going on to the tiller. His grandfather tells him to make for the shore. The boy protests.

'What's up?' Jochen says.

'We haven't got any fish. The boy's just reminding me. We were about to drop the nets when we saw you.'

'Don't rush on my account. A sea voyage would be a nice break.' Jochen jerks his thumb at the dead American,. 'He doesn't mind.'

Jochen is leaning in the doorway, exhausted. The grandfather studies him and shakes his head.

'We've got to get you ashore, *Hauptmann*. You need tucking up somewhere warm and dry.'

'Get that jacket off him. They're very warm,' Jochen tells him and, 'more cartridges in the leg pocket,' when the grandfather unbuckles the gun belt and pulls it from under the corpse.

Bruno, Jochen knows the grandfather's name now, cuts some of the parachute shrouds and ties the corpse securely to the deck. He slips a sack over the head so the boy, Klaus Peter, won't have to look at the immobile white face.

Bruno gives Jochen trousers and a sweater. His toes return fully and his fingers, too. Wrapped up in the blankets, he sleeps.

A distant aero engine wakes him. It gets louder, closer. He struggles up from below.

A Gustav dives on the boat. He waves with both arms. The Gustav turns. It's less than a hundred metres up. Flaps down it flies towards them slowly. Jochen waves. It must be one of the guys. They'll have split the area up, one part each. He reads the number but can't remember whose regular machine it is. The Gustav circles, rocks its wings and climbs away.

They share cheese and black bread. Delicious. Bruno gives him the rest of the brandy. The boat rises and falls. In the troughs he can see nothing but water through the porthole.

'How did you find me in this swell?'

'I climbed the mast and called out directions to Grandpa, Herr Hauptmann.'

Jochen rubs the boy's hair. 'Thanks, K P. And call me Jochen.'

'I can't, sir.'

'I won't talk to you if you don't.'

They get back early in the evening. Bruno rings, makes arrangements about the corpse and offers Jochen a bed for the night. He accepts. He'll go back tomorrow. They eat. Fish stew. Hearty and scrumptious. Bruno's wife fusses over him. His uniform hangs on chairs by the fire to dry. Klaus Peter's father is in E-boats on the channel coast. His mother is dead. Jochen doesn't ask how.

People drop in with bottles. Jochen, with his Diamonds, clearly adds to Bruno's status.

There's a piano. Jochen plays.

'What was that thing you were singing when we found you?' Bruno says.

'*J'attendrai*. It's French. It means 'I will wait'.'

He plays and sings. They don't mind that it's in French. But they all know the German version, *Komm zuruck*. Someone else plays and they all sing that.

Later, wrapped in several blankets, he sleeps a deep, dreamless, uninterrupted sleep until the morning sounds of the house wake him.

Klaus Peter walks him from the village to the main road and he hitches a ride on a Wehrmacht truck, then another to the railway. When he gets back, the guys have just taken off. Schaefer is leading. Jochen can hear the distant sound of many engines, the faraway crump of flak.

A bath, a shave, clean clothes, vile coffee and he feels back to normal. His Ami jacket is stiff and clogged with salt. Scholz says he'll find someone to sort it out along with his uniform. Jochen asks him to get hold of a print of one of his publicity photos, too.

He goes into his office and sits down. Nothing's been moved. There's the letter, unread, and the photo where he dropped it when the phone rang. He picks it up. Turns it. There's writing.

Ilse, aged five months.

He grabs the letter. Reads it swiftly. Devours it. Then reads it again more carefully.

Darling Jochen...

The phone rings. He snatches it up. It can't be important, there's already a raid.

'Give me ten minutes,' he says.

Darling Jochen,

I don't know if this will reach you but of course if you're reading it, it has. That's a silly sentence. The truth is I'm nervous about writing. I don't know how you'll take this sudden news. The baby in the photograph is our daughter, Ilse. I never particularly ever wanted a baby but now Ilse is here it's clear she was my life's purpose. She lies beside me now, sleeping, and so beautiful. I need nothing from you, Jochen. I'm writing because you have the right to know of your daughter's existence. You may tell the world, or you may tell no one. Forgive me for the name. It was the only one I could possibly choose. I know your Ilse was your precious one. Now Ilse is mine.

Uwe's friends have been wonderful. I work for them as a kind of maid or housekeeper, although recently I've been less able to do so, of course, though I'm picking up my duties again now. They have secured status for me as a Jewish refugee from persecution. I believe they care for me. And they dote on Ilse.

I have told several lies here. The worst is that I am your Jewish wife whom you were unable safely to acknowledge and had to get out of Germany. I selfishly believed that that lie would ease my way here. It pains me to deceive them and to take your name that has not been given to me. I'm afraid I told so many lies while I was surviving back home in Germany that they come very easily to me now. I beg your forgiveness for that huge lie, you who have given me this life here.

If you are married now, then I wish you and Lotte a happy, happy life. I wish it also for your mother, of whom I have such fond memories of that day she helped me.

You must feel no obligation to me or Ilse. You have already given us everything and I believe we can live a good life in this good country.

You are a wonderful man, Jochen. If I believed and if I ever prayed, I would pray for you constantly. Since I don't, I can only say to you, 'Stay alive. Stay alive.'

Please accept a fond and loving kiss from me and from your daughter Ilse, who, if she knew you, would also love you.

Yours in deepest gratitude,

Gerda x x

He stares at the wall. He's stunned. Overcome.

Eight of the fourteen Schaefer took off with make it back home. One guy wipes his undercarriage off while landing but climbs out safely. Schaefer's got two Mustangs. Everyone else is happy just to have escaped. Jochen doesn't blame Schaefer. He would have done no better himself. You can't take puppies out and expect them to hunt like wolfhounds.

'Why?' he says to Jonny Beck on the phone, when Jonny says there'll be replacements arriving in the morning.

'Don't you want them?'

'I'd be tempted to shoot them as they get off the truck. At least we'd save their Gustavs.'

'You're mad.'

'I'm angry. None of them can fly properly. Take us out of the line for a few weeks. Bring us up to strength and post us somewhere safe from Mustangs so I can teach them to fly.'

'I can't do that. Who'd shoot them down while you're all gone?'

'Who's shooting them down now? Not us.'

'I can't give that order. I'd be court-martialled.'

Jochen slams down the phone but picks it up again a moment later. Using his hero of the Reich voice, he gets passed on a couple of times and in four minutes General Galland answers.

'Murville! What do you want? Another dinner at the Adlon?'

'If only, sir…' He tells Galland his idea.

Galland laughs. 'You've got a nerve!'

'Probably, but I won't have a *gruppe* tomorrow otherwise.'

The order arrives by telegram the next morning.

The transports leave first with the ground crews, but not in their habitual black overalls today; spic and span instead in uniforms, as if for inspection. The Gustavs catch them up and fly escort for the final ten minutes. They're not far from the Swiss border. Snow-topped mountains just a quick flight away; get lost, pilot error, and alight in the land of chocolate and cuckoo clocks.

They start work early the next day. He wants everyone up three or four times. New boys do circuits and bumps to practise landings, into the wind first, then crosswind. The old hands mentor the new ones. He flies with everyone. He escapes from attacks then chases them in turn. He puts on a slow flying show, flaps and wheels down, and makes each of them do the same. The handful who know how teach the others bad weather flying. To practise in poor visibility, they take off late and land with the light almost gone. They chase each other in spiral climbs. They borrow a couple of Heinkels and crews and practise attacks; from the front and the rear, from above and below. He sends them up in pairs and has them fly at each other at 450 kilometres per hour, nine hundred combined, to get an appreciation of the approach speeds they'll experience against the Ami heavies and the short time they'll have to fire. To teach them to get about, he sends them off with a map and a set route, back in an hour. In the evenings they eat, drink, sing; a big group of pals. It's a training camp. It's a holiday.

Snowdrops are over, but primroses and daffodils are in verges and banks. Far away from here, it's Ilse's first spring. Gerda will be showing her all this. Telling her the names in German? Or learning the Swedish first herself to tell Ilse in what will be her native tongue?

In their temporary office, he and Scholz share a desk. Scholz calls him 'boss', he calls Scholz 'uncle'. He's twice Jochen's age; an observer in the Great War, one eye gone and now a *leutnant* with no desire for greater rank. His wife and daughter are nurses in Bonn, far from the Ivans' approach. Calm, quiet, efficient, with a beautiful light tenor voice. Jochen's accompanied him a couple times after dinner as he sings Schubert. The guys listened respectfully and applauded. Only one song each time, though. No sense in trying anyone's patience.

Scholz has found a photograph of Jochen with the diamonds at his throat; very stirring and inspiring. He writes across it:

For my friend, Klaus Peter, Prince of look outs! With eternal gratitude for my life. And to Bruno, good health and may you always have a fine catch! Jochen Murville, Hauptmann.

Three weeks in, they're restricted to one flight a day. Fuel shortage. Then they're grounded, waiting for a delivery. Training is way down the priority list.

'Don't they care?' he yells at Scholz in the privacy of their office. 'These kids need to be flying!' He kicks the wall by the door. Plaster falls off. 'Am I supposed to lead them all up to be killed? I feel like a murderer. Who's in charge of fuel? What idiot's organising it all?'

'The usual one, I expect, boss.'

Scholz's quiet tone stops him short. He's embarrassed. Scholz wears an eye patch, looks like a pirate, but never behaves like one.

'Sorry, uncle.'

He gets on the phone and to no avail pesters everyone he can think of about the fuel situation.

The 9th of April. Easter Day. Scholz has found a church that those who want to can attend. There are no padres in Goering's Luftwaffe. Jochen joins the service. Nostalgia overcomes him. Ilse would have been in the choir today at their church raising her voice to God. He can almost hear her. He catches Scholz eyeing him and pulls himself together by thinking of Lotte.

There's lamb for lunch but before that, Schaefer calls for everyone's attention. Jochen looks round and sees a brightly coloured box in Schaefer's hands.

'Happy Easter, boss!' Schaefer thrusts the box at him. At Schaefer's urging they've all raided their emergency survival rations for chocolate and the most skilful of their cooks, who once did this sort of thing for a living, has come up with the goods: several painted eggs, blown and filled with hazelnut chocolate lying on tissue paper. Jochen's astonished and can only grin at them all.

Back in the north, new Gustavs have arrived with a methane injection system that greatly improves acceleration. They fly against the Amis three or four times a week. His *gruppe* can take off and land safely now. Flying accidents have ceased but on every sortie they lose one or two to Mustangs and Thunderbolts. Replacements arrive who are barely trained and the old problems begin to reappear. He does what he can for them on a front-line airfield: training flights between raids when they're safe from marauding fighters; practice with the veterans. It's not much. Jochen despairs.

He reads Willi's letter again and as an antidote to the image of Dr Hofmann, who looms like an ogre in his mind, he reads Gerda's letter and studies the photograph of her and Ilse. His daughter. He'll be twenty-four soon and what are his achievements? He's fathered a daughter he's never seen, and he's killed many, many men.

An invasion seems imminent. The Allies will certainly come straight across to the Pas-de-Calais. Rommel has been building defences. The rumour Jochen hears suggests they'll be sent to France to oppose the landings. And what about the bombers currently flattening Germany?

His mother writes. Lilo's mother-in-law has invited her to stay in the country with them, far from the bombs. But she can't leave Rolf and, more importantly, she needs to be on hand in case he manages a couple of days leave and dashes home to marry Lotte. More despair. He won't be marrying Lotte, but he needs to make it clear. Tell Lotte. He's leaving his mother in danger!

An order comes through sending him to Lechfeld to try out the Me 262. He gets on the phone to protest. How can he leave his guys? They have replacements every day. He refuses to send them up against the Amis until he's given them a few more hours in the air. Schaefer, if he's the one to stand in for Jochen, won't have the status to resist Jonny Beck or anyone higher up the chain. His protest is denied, and he flies south.

Lechfeld. Near Augsburg. The Messerschmitt works. A long concrete runway. Not so good for a Gustav that really needs a grass field where you can always land into the wind.

The Alps are in view again; gateway to the Swiss land of plenty. He turns away and into the wind and lands on the grass beside the runway. He taxis past a 262, the plane he's come to fly. It's dangerous-looking, shark-like, an engine beneath each wing, without propellers but with a nose wheel that aligns the fuselage parallel to the ground, as if already in flight, giving the machine a ready-for-action look. There are others hidden in shelters around the airfield.

Nowotny is forming the first 262 unit at Lechfeld. He hopes to be in action in two or three weeks but: 'The engines only last a few hours. Ten, twelve if you're lucky. Then they need changing. It's not really ready yet.'

'Still,' Jochen says, 'it's fast.'

'But acceleration is very slow on take-off and you have to open up really carefully or the engine will flame out and then you've had it.'

'Does it glide?'

'Like a brick.'

'We'll learn how to use it.'

'I hope so. What we need is guys who've had a year or two on Gustavs and 190s. But they're all spread out on alarm start duty.'

'It's fast, though. They'll never catch us.'

'Unless they lurk over our bases and attack when we're coming in at one seventy with a cup of fuel left. That's what I'd do.'

'We'll have to patrol the fields with Gustavs.'

'Where will they come from?'

Jochen is silent.

'Sorry,' Nowotny says. 'I don't mean to drown your enthusiasm. You haven't even flown it yet.'

'Does Fatty know all this?'

'Who knows what he knows? Hitler wanted it as a bomber but...'

'A bomber!'

'Yes. To get revenge, apparently, but they managed to kill that idea.'

After dinner they drink a few brandies and tell stories of dead comrades. Lying in bed, he imagines the discussion he's planning with Dr Hofmann in a week's time. He's been granted two days leave in Berlin at the end of his Lechfeld week. Lotte will expect to be getting married but there's going to be a big row instead.

With the Alps in the far distance, one of Messerschmitt's engineers shows him around the 262. He won't answer Jochen's questions about the engine, too secret for him. The Schwalbe, they're calling it. A good name for a jet, a swallow being such a fast, darting bird.

'Gently with the throttle,' the guy tells him. He climbs in, straps up, parachute first, though how you'd get out at nine hundred is anyone's guess. A functional cockpit, dials and taps well-laid out and easy to see and grab, though the board they all sit in is plywood painted black. Plywood! In the world's most modern aeroplane. But the view! There's no long nose tipped up in front. You can see everything, see what to avoid. It'll be a treat to taxi. But he doesn't taxi. To save jet fuel, there's a tractor to tow him to the end of the runway.

They start the engines. No vibration. And the sound! Not a roar, more a low whistle. The Schwalbe rocks against the brakes. He drops the canopy and waves the chocks away.

Through the crackle in his ears his remote instructor talks him through everything.

'Open the throttle slowly, three centimetres,' he hears.

He feels a gentle push in his back as his bird starts to roll. No vibration! So strange.

'Another three centimetres.'

He obeys and he's pushed harder into his seat. He glances at the speedo. 110 already. No movement in the machine but through the wheels comes a regular jolt from the joins in the runway concrete.

'Another three.'

She feels lighter. 170. Very light. No concrete joins now. He's off.

'OK. Wheels up.'

He feels them clunk into the wings and the nose.

'Open up fully. Climb at forty degrees. Level off at three thousand and fly. Check the speed.'

Three thousand. He's there already! He puts the stick forwards. Level flight! Six hundred, seven hundred, eight, eight-fifty, nine hundred!

'Nine hundred! Whee!'

'Calm down, cowboy! Slow down a bit and do some turns. Enjoy yourself!'

He does. It's a revelation. Galland was right. There's an angel pushing him. And protecting him. No one will hit him at this speed.

His time up, he puts the nose down and closes the throttle a little. Ground features grow larger. He joins the circuit and commits to the landing. The Schwalbe flies down at one seventy. Now he feels he's in danger as Nowotny suggested; the throttle takes effect so slowly. If he had to open up to escape Ami fighters, he'd hit the ground before the Schwalbe could accelerate. He touches down and rolls. Steering with the nose wheel, he swings to the left, off the runway. The view is so good it's like driving a car.

The Schwalbe is everything it's cracked up to be. But tricky. That throttle. Open it too fast and the engine might flame out or catch fire. But there'll be a thousand of them by Christmas! God help the Amis and the English. But who's going to fly them? Where will the pilots come from? And where do the guys come from on the assembly line?

No one says. That's as big a secret as the Jumo 004 engine.

He puts in hours on the Schwalbe. He loves it but he doesn't look forward to landing one after a fight. He shakes his head at Nowotny.

'Wonderful. But too late.'

Berlin from the air is a sight to break his heart. Buildings flattened. Only shells of others remaining. Piles of rubble. Groups clearing roads so traffic can pass. Craters. Upside-down, burnt-out vehicles. The whole pattern repeated into the distance as far as he can see.

He lands at Tempelhof, following the line indicated between bomb craters. He grabs his bag from the hatch behind his seat and leaves his Gustav for two days. The S-Bahn is still running. He takes it.

His street has not escaped. Gaps have appeared in the avenue of limes where trees have gone; buildings further up, too. What must it have been like as it was happening? He starts running up the stairs but slows to a walk after one flight. His left leg. It still hurts on occasion. No one's in. He gets the key from the usual neighbour. She hugs his arm and says he looks exhausted. He finds some cheese, makes coffee and falls asleep on the sofa.

His mother wakes him. She's excited. He hasn't warned her of his arrival. He hasn't told Lotte, either. He didn't want any arrangements made. His mother tells him to go and find Lotte at once but he sits her down and explains to her why there'll be no marriage. She's shocked. She cries. Shakes her head, tut-tuts, mutters, 'Oh, dear, oh, dear.' But she doesn't try to change his mind.

He takes the S-Bahn again as far as he can and ends his journey on foot. He's nervous. He'll have to play it by ear. It might be dangerous for Willi if Jochen reveals what Willi's told him. He needs to wheedle the information out of Lotte's father without letting on that he knows anything. It must appear to be a discovery, a surprise, a terrible shock to Jochen.

The receptionist directs him through the hospital corridors. A middle-aged woman in a white coat opens the door he knocks on. She's clearly taken aback but in the same instant puts two and two together.

'Hauptmann Murville! Dr Hofmann will be delighted. This way please. He's only been back from the East for a couple of days.'

Hofmann must have heard. He comes from a further room.

'Jochen, my boy. What a great delight to see you!' He pumps Jochen's hand. 'You look tired, though. Fräulein Knoke, some coffee.' The woman in the white coat leaves.

Dr Hofmann shows him into his own room. Dark oak shelves stuffed full of books, gold leaf titles on leather; other shelves with skulls; assorted human bones; glass jars of alcohol, each containing a different medical horror. Jochen looks away from them at the papers piled on Hofmann's desk.

Dr Hofmann smiles. 'To what do I owe the honour, Jochen?'

'Well, I've often found myself curious about your work and just now I realised I was passing. So I thought...'

'Why not? Of course. An opportunity. Always grab them! Though two days earlier and you wouldn't have found me. I was far from here, in our new eastern territories.'

'Poland?'

Hofmann laughs. 'They used to call it that.'

'Warsaw?'

'No. What you might call... a small research station.'

'I suppose science is at home everywhere.'

'Exactly.'

'What are you researching?'

'The differences between people.'

'Oh.'

'You know my field is eugenics, don't you?'

'I don't think I did.'

Hofmann laughs. 'You and Lotte have got better things to discuss than the old man's work, eh?'

Biscuits and coffee arrive.

'Can't you study people in Berlin?'

'Not in the same way.'

'Dr Hofmann, I spent my youth playing the piano. I studied just enough to get into the Luftwaffe Academy and since then I've been flying planes. I'm afraid I don't really know what eugenics is.'

Hofmann laughs. 'Eugenicists are interested in how different races compare.'

'In what ways?'

'Biology, anatomy, lengths of bones, for example, skull size, too, and, therefore, brain size.'

'But aren't there always quite big differences among people? Eye, hair colour? Tall, short? In my unit, for example, we're all different sizes and shapes.'

'Of course. But all of you must be basically good Aryan stock. You have no degenerates there.'

'You mean Jews.'

Hofmann laughs. 'And don't forget negroes, gypsies, homosexuals. Mental defectives! Eugenics makes plain their inferiority and the superiority of Aryans. That's the beauty of it.'

'Remarkable. And you study all that in your research station?'

'Yes. It's a wonderful by-product of our policy of shipping human detritus east. All conveniently gathered together.'

'In a camp? That's your research station?'

Hofmann nods. 'Auschwitz. Dr Mengele's in charge there. A brilliant mind. His paper on the human jaw and what we can learn from it is groundbreaking. I'm fortunate to be an associate of his.'

Jochen doesn't have to wheedle, a mere attentive gaze seems to suffice.

'I'm so very pleased you dropped in, Jochen. I've sometimes thought, you know, that you might not entirely agree with the Führer's teachings. You're an artistic type, you see. You know nothing of science. I've often wondered if you'd have sympathy with my work. Well, I'm glad you clearly do. Let me give you a brief rundown.'

Dr Hofmann is quite full of himself, warms to his subject. Perhaps his work really does excite him. This must be what Willi's had to listen to, what prompted the letter he sent. Jochen feels a little light-headed, thinks he might be trembling. Hofmann continues with the description of his work: studying mongrel races in order to understand the German race. Differences in anatomy and biology are small but key in proving the superiority of heredity over environment; in proving the genetic superiority of the German race and finding the route to increasing the rate of reproduction.

Jochen's throat has gone dry. He takes a sip from his cup. The coffee's cold now and bitter.

Twins! Jewish twins! Mengele selects the ones for study himself. Twins are extremely useful! For comparisons! Experiments! Amputations of limbs! Injections of typhus! In one twin. To compare.

'How do you make the comparisons?'

'Examine their organs.'

Hofmann notices Jochen's puzzlement. 'We usually

euthanise them first, of course, before we remove the organ.'

Usually! Jochen stands abruptly. His chair scrapes back, tips over and lands with a crash.

Dr Hofmann looks startled.

'You cut organs out of living people?'

Dr Hofmann stares at him.

'How are the people in this camp occupied?'

'They work if they're able.'

'And if not?'

'We can't feed them forever if they're unproductive. Dr Mengele often makes the selections himself.'

'What selections?' Has he shouted?

'My dear boy, don't be naïve. I'd hate to think my daughter was marrying a naïve person.'

'You execute them.'

'You don't execute vermin.'

'They're exterminated.'

Hofmann gives a little smile.

'I'm going.'

He has a buzzing in his head. He feels he might vomit. At the door, he turns. Hofmann is staring at him.

'I was a twin,' he shouts.

He's waited till he thinks Lotte will be home. He found a bar open that had some schnapps but that didn't calm the frenzy in his head. Everything he's feared since the party two years ago, when he overheard those officers discussing the planned liquidation of the Jews, is true. And Mengele and Hofmann are an extra unexpected horror, though already disclosed to him in Willi's letter. Beside him is the slot in the door frame that first told him this had been a Jewish house, that first cast a doubt in his mind about Lotte.

A footstep and the door swings open. Lotte. Tired but as beautiful as ever. He sees her thoughts blossom on her face in an instant. Jochen! Loved one! Wedding! Husband! She flings her arms around his neck and kisses him. He takes her shoulders and almost lifts her away from him.

'We must talk.'

'Of course.'

'Who is it?' her mother calls and appears. 'Jochen, darling.' She beams at him. 'How wonderful!'

'Excuse us,' he says to Frau Hofmann. 'In here?' He opens the first door on the right. He's never seen it before. An austere room that a maid might show a caller into when she goes to ask if the family is at home. He half pulls Lotte in and closes the door behind them.

'Jochen, what is it? What's the matter? Has something happened?'

'I have to talk about your father, Lotte. Do you know where he's just come back from?'

'Somewhere east, I think. Observing a colleague's work.'

'What sort of work?'

'Something to do with eugenics. It's all a bit over my head. Anna has a much better idea. Ask her. Jochen, you haven't kissed me yet.'

He ignores her. 'Let me tell you what he told me.'

'Did you go to see him? I'm glad. You should be on good terms.'

'This colleague. Name of Mengele.'

'Oh, that's right, he mentioned his name.'

'He's a very nice man.'

'Most of father's colleagues are.'

'Lotte!'

'What?' She begins to realise something may be seriously amiss. Her smile has gone.

'Let me tell you what his work consists of.'

'What?'

'He studies people.'

'Well?'

'He studies twins in particular because the comparisons are so useful.'

'I suppose they might be.'

'For example, first he infects one of them with typhus and then he compares them afterwards. He compares their organs. He takes them out to do it.'

Lotte is staring at him.

'Of course, he kills them first. Usually.'

'Who are these people?'

'Jews, negroes, gypsies, the disabled, queers.'

'Queers? What's that?'

'Lotte! Homosexuals.'

'Perverts, then.'

'They're humans first.'

'But Jochen, all these people are degenerates.'

'The Party calls them that. But your father says these people are so similar to Aryans that we can learn from these studies and improve the German race.'

'There you are, then.'

'But if we're so similar that we can learn about ourselves, then how are they degenerates? How are they different from us?'

'Look at them. You can tell. Jews, negroes. It's clear.'

'A Jew taught me to play the piano. My friend in Africa is a negro. He saved the boss's life.'

'I don't understand, Jochen.'

'This man, Mengele, selects twins to work on in this camp. Auschwitz. Selects them personally, in this hell hole where the healthy work and the rest are exterminated. Twins, Lotte. I was a twin.'

'But you and Ilse, that's different.'

'Huh. Your father agrees with you. He admires Mengele. A great man, he thinks. What do you think?'

'If my father thinks he's a great man, then he must be.'

'What about all this stuff I've just told you?'

'I don't know about any of that. It's not my concern.'

'You're a German. These are your people.'

'Jochen. Don't take all this to heart so. You're not a scientist, dealing in facts. You don't live that life. You're an artist.'

'I'm a murderer, Lotte. But I don't tie anyone down and butcher them to examine the bits.'

'Why are you saying all this?'

'Lotte, I can't marry you.'

'But you love me. You told me.'

He stares at her.

'You don't love me. Oh. Were you always lying?'

'I loved you. But then I came to realise you believe all this Nazi garbage. And even now I can't alter what you think, can I? How could we live together? We'd be miserable. We'd hate each other.'

She stares at him, stares into his eyes. He stares back. She screams and falls back into an armchair, finally overpowered by his words, puts her hands over her face and screams and screams. He doesn't know what to do. The door bursts open and her mother is there, very agitated.

'What's happened? What is it? Lotte? Jochen?'

'Lotte will tell you. You won't believe me.'

Frau Hofmann goes to comfort Lotte who's sobbing now. Jochen leaves. He pulls the front door closed, runs down the steps and at the bottom realises he hasn't got his cap.

It's inside on the table in that room. What to do? He looks up at the door. How can he go back? He can't just ring the bell. As he turns to go, the door opens a crack and his cap flies out. Flung out like a piece of rubbish as he imagines he would have been if he hadn't left. He picks up the cap and starts the walk home.

What will happen now? A suit of breach of promise? Denunciation to the Gestapo for refusing to accept Nazi racial beliefs? He'll just have to wait and see. Who cares, anyway? At least he won't be trapped in that family.

7

The Allies are ashore. In Normandy! What happened to the Pas-de-Calais? So much for their strategic and tactical experts. He gathers the guys together and tells them.

'They're ashore in numbers, more every day, apparently. Amis, English, Canadians. And French. I imagine we'll be sent somewhere closer.'

Meantime, most days there are the usual concentrations in sector Dora-Dora. They go up and do their best until they're ordered south. Back to France again. Just north of Paris. But there's no time for tourist visits.

He's stopped counting his score and Jurg no longer paints bars on the rudder of his Gustav.

One day, Beck rings. Jochen doesn't see Jonny very often, which is quite often enough.

'Congratulations!'

'On what?'

'You've got two hundred.'

'Cigarettes?'

'Victories, idiot.'

'How do you know?'

'Someone further up counts them. They sent the message down. There's talk of another decoration.'

'What decoration?'

'I don't know. Perhaps they'll invent one for you. I expect the Führer will want to present you with it.'

Oh, maybe he will.

'You go for me, Jonny. I know you'd love to have him breathe in your face.'

'Don't be disrespectful!'

'I only said it to irritate you.'

'Well, you shouldn't have. You're in big trouble.'

'Oh, yeah?'

'Some Gestapo guy rang me, trying to track you down.'

'Gestapo? What have I done now?'

It's a toss-up, of course. Which is it? Disrespect of Nazi ideology or the death of Anton Heinecke?

'Only bumped off a Gestapo agent, wait for it, who happened to be this guy's brother.'

'What?'

'Exactly. Well, though I'd pay money to watch them interrogate you, I told him to fuck off. I said, "Why would a highly-decorated hero of the Reich, personally known to the Führer, and my most-valued officer, be murdering Gestapo agents?"'

'Most-valued?'

'Of course. If you weren't there, your *gruppe's* score would fall to practically nothing. It's only the truth, though I nearly choked saying it.'

'I'm deeply touched, Jonny. I must send you a gift.

What about my treasured copy of the *Moonlight Sonata* played by Schnabel, the top Jew?'

'Send it. I'll look forward to stamping on it!'

Heinecke's still investigating, then. And got more information by the sound of it. He hopes no one's had pressure put on them. Otto, for example, or Uwe. Or Rolf. His mother!

He's had no contact with Lotte since that evening and no contact with her father, either. Hofmann! He can't call him doctor any longer. Doctors are like Dr Feinstein, kind and caring but in his case, long disappeared. Exterminated.

Did zu Sayn-Wittgenstein know anything about the camps? He never mentioned them. He only said that Hitler was a rabid, incompetent fanatic who was dragging Germany into an abyss that the army could still drag the country out of if set free from the Führer's directives. He'd be doing his military duty by shooting him, Heinrich said. Jochen's not interested in military duty. If he did the act, it would be to eliminate the chief barbarian.

Jochen still has the Beretta. Could he smuggle it in with him if they came up with a further decoration for him? If Hitler decided to present it and have one of those private chinwags he so loves to have with his boys? A couple of very big 'ifs' and he can do nothing to affect the process. Except, perhaps, by raising his score and making the decoration more likely.

They're at one thousand. No sun, total cloud cover. He's leading a patrol of four to find ground strafing English or Ami fighters looking for panzers to blast with their rockets.

They're not high enough to spot much. The allies rule the sky, and this patrol is next to suicide.

'Three o'clock. Edge of the wood.' Schaefer's voice through the crackle.

'Victor, victor,' he calls as he turns.

There they are. Three Typhoons queueing up to follow their leader, who's just blasted the wood. Must be a bunch of tanks in there. A quick glance around, nothing.

'After us, Blue One.'

The leader has zoomed up over the wood and is turning to watch his guys.

The rear Typhoon fills Jochen's sight. He fires and sparkles hit all around the cockpit. The plane goes straight in and explodes in a meadow. The two attacking Typhoons break right and left, obviously warned by their leader. He fires ahead of the one going left. The engine begins to smoke, and the Typhoon starts a climb, making height for a jump.

Jochen leaves him and looks around. Nothing, no one. Where's the Typhoon leader?

'Jochen, break right.' Flo's voice, his wing-man.

His turn is instantaneous. He drops his flaps to turn tighter. He's pushed firmly into his seat. Typhoons are fast but fly on rails. To his right as he turns, with the Gustav's wings perpendicular to the earth, he sees woods and then meadow and then woods. He looks back as well as he can in his Gustav but sees nothing.

'What's happening, Flo?'

No answer.

'Anybody there?'

No answer.

Time to get out of there.

He rolls out upside down and dives for the woods. He pulls out just above the trees and makes a turn for his course home. He opens the throttle to full and climbs, does a full turn to check behind, nothing, then heads for the clouds.

There's a tremendous bang followed at once by clattering noises and smoke in the cockpit. He switches off. Flames appear from the engine. They blow back over the canopy.

Out! The canopy flies away. Straps off, helmet off. He straightens the Gustav up and tips himself out. A light green, dark green patchwork below as he tumbles: meadow and woodland. The chute jerks him upright and he floats down towards the grass. The earth shudders through him as he lands. He manages to turn and roll as the manual says but there's a sharp pain in his left ankle as he does so. He pulls off the straps and gathers the chute up.

He feels exposed. He's a hundred metres from the trees. With the bundled chute in his arms, he runs for them as best he can. Every step shoots a pain through his ankle. He pushes in under drooping branches. Beeches, he registers, without thinking. He drops the chute and sits on it, looks around as he gets his breath back. No trace of him left in the field he's run from. No sign of his Gustav. No explosion, no bullets going off in the distance that he can hear. In the wood, just trees, so thick it's like twilight beneath them; no paths, no clearings. He hasn't a clue where he is. He's lost his bearings in those final few hectic moments of the fight. He's probably down on the Allied side. He saw no planes when the engine was hit, no flak burst either, but it could have been a truly lucky first time shot. So, which way home?

He holds his ankle through his boot, but he doesn't dare take the boot off, it'd never go back on. He's wearing an old pair of desert issue trousers. They're cooler for the summer and since the invasion they never fly high enough to get cold and, he's only recently admitted it to himself, he thinks they're lucky. He pulls the trousers out of his boots and tugs them down over the tops. He's wearing his Ami jacket with the stars on the shoulders. He leaves his side cap where it is in an inside pocket. He doesn't know who he'll meet first. He wipes a hand over his face and his wrist touches the diamonds at his throat. He pulls them off and tucks them in a pocket. He undoes his shirt collar. Sam Levine's Browning is in its holster on his right hip. He takes it out, arms it with a bullet up the spout, just in case, puts on the safety-catch and slides it back in the holster.

He pushes himself up. Pressure on his left foot is very painful for his ankle. He hobbles around and finds a straightish length of broken branch a metre and a half long. He holds it as a staff in his left hand. He feels like Moses but leaning on it relieves the pain just enough. He begins to make his way through the wood in what he feels is the direction to the German lines, and anyway, he can't go out into the open meadow behind him.

There's a path going more or less in his direction. It runs into the distance with trees arched over it. It's very inviting but he crosses it quickly and puts several trees between him and the path before turning again to follow its direction. Birds are singing. Building nests? Too late in the year. Taking food back to their young. Real life goes on while men kill each other.

He knows he's making quite a row, pushing through undergrowth, crunching twigs underfoot, but what can he do about it?

He hears a voice. And another. He stands motionless with a tree between him and the sound. It's French. He sees two faces, unshaven, one with a beret above it. He steps out with his free hand held high, the other still on the staff.

'*Bonjour,*' he calls. Two Sten guns swing round. Shit! He didn't see them.

Resistance!

'*Qui est la?*'

'*M'aidez!*' he calls again.

'*C'est un americain,*' he hears.

'Yeah, American,' he says in the best Hollywood imitation he can manage. 'Where are the Americans?'

He hobbles towards them.

'*Comment?*'

'The Americans?' He points around, raises his shoulders and his hands, shrugs.

'*La!*' One of the guys points in the direction he's come from. Shit! He'll have to turn round with them here watching.

'And the Germans?'

'*Les Boches?*' The man spits. '*La!*' He points the way Jochen was walking.

'OK,' Jochen says and turns away from them. Perhaps they'll let him be on his way if he's walking towards the Amis. '*Merci,*' he says over his shoulder.

He hears them talking. '*Mais, c'était un Boche qui est tombé!*' Then a command, '*Arrêtez!*'

He slides behind a tree, draws the Browning and flicks off the safety. He hears them running at him. He puts his head round the tree and fires at the nearest man. A terrible noise in the quiet woods. The man goes down. His shoulder, Jochen thinks. The Sten gun has fallen from the man's hands. The other man is struggling with his gun. It won't fire.

Jochen's heard that Stens often jam. He aims the Browning at the man's head and limps up to him. Jochen holds his left hand out.

'*S'il vous plait.*'

The man passes over the Sten.

Jochen goes over to the wounded man. He's sitting up, his right arm covered in blood. It hangs down.

'*Ça va?*'

The man shrugs with one shoulder.

Jochen picks up the other Sten gun. He tucks both under his left arm.

'*Ici,*' he calls to the other man. '*Aidez votre ami!*'

Jochen backs away as the man approaches and keeps the Browning levelled at him.

From thirty metres away he says, '*Je suis désolé, monsieur. Mais, c'est la guerre. Bon chance.*'

He heads in the direction of the German lines. Hopes they didn't lie. He takes the magazine off the jammed

Sten, puts it in his pocket and slings the gun as far as he can into the undergrowth to his right. He hangs the other gun round his neck, hoping it won't jam if he needs it. He limps on. His ankle pain, which the excitement drove away, is back. He's lost his staff but finds another. Half an hour later, he hears German voices. He throws the Sten away, puts on his Diamonds and his side cap, takes off his Ami jacket, turns it inside out to hide the stars and calls out, 'German pilot coming in! Don't shoot! German pilot! Hauptmann Murville!'

His ankle is only a sprain, but the doc grounds him. He protests but when he sits in a Gustav and kicks the rudder bar, he knows he can't fly it yet.

He hobbles around with a stick and talks to the ground crews. They work all hours and never complain. Not one of them has ever got a medal. The Doc tells him to stop wandering about and rest his ankle. It's the only cure. He capitulates. He doesn't want to delay his return to the air.

He sits sideways at his desk with his bad ankle raised on another chair. He has long periods for rumination. His life's in chaos. Just like Germany. That camp Hofmann talked about! Are they all like that? How many are there? And the Jews and all the other poor devils. He knows about them now. He has evidence, he's heard testimony. He's guilty, too, if he does nothing. But what can he do? And all decided on by a gang of vicious crooks, who are running the country into the ground. Bandits, Heinrich called them, as well, in one of their long, fairly drunken conversations. Not a good family amongst the lot of them.

Goering, a dope fiend, Goebbels, a slimy lying rat, Himmler, an evil inhuman swine. But what can you expect with a failed artist who looks like a music hall comedian in charge? An Austrian corporal! How did he get to hold sway? They should be put in front of a firing squad one after the other, starting with the comedian. Then a general could take over. One with a bit of sense. Rommel?

Heinrich's dead now, though. But Jochen's got his pistol. Could he? Really? If he managed to get the Beretta in with him? Bullet up the spout ready, hand into tunic pocket, safety off, slide out the gun, stick it into his stomach, one, two, three, four, as many shots as he could get off before they jumped on him. If they were having one of those private chinwags and people had to run in from another room, he might manage one to Hitler's head, too.

He'd be shot dead on the spot. Or viciously beaten up and then shot. Or guillotined or hanged. Not nice. But his future anyway is probably death in some terrible form or other. Burning up in his Gustav or torn apart by bullets from a Mustang's guns. If he shot Hitler, he'd be notorious. Or renowned, perhaps, if things go on as they are, and the Allies write the history.

His mother would be sure to suffer though. She brought him up badly, they'd say. She'd be as guilty as him in their minds. All that piano playing she encouraged. Taught by a Jew! What true German mother would arrange that for her son? She was as bad as him. She was behind his deranged actions. She was as much an assassin as her son. She must join him on the scaffold. How can he do that to her?

A letter and a package arrive. The package is from Berlin, but he doesn't recognise the writing, the letter is from his mother and the postmark is Neunerstadt! She's gone there! He wrote again and urged her to, since there was no wedding to stick around for. He lights a cigarette, leans back and enjoys his mother's chatty news.

It's like a letter from the old days, before all the tragedy and the bombing horrors. It's like being back at school, she says, with an all-female household, chatting and gossiping all day and no staff left since they've all gone to war work of different kinds. It's a big house to keep clean but they all pitch in, sweeping, dusting, beating carpets, singing the old songs together on wash day, taking turns to cook and with country ingredients they eat really very well. Vicky Deichmann is an old friend, of course, and Lilo's mother-in-law is a good sort, one of the old school. She likes her immensely. She does so hope Lilo's husband is surviving and makes it home eventually. Little Andreas keeps Lilo very busy but he's such a darling, it's wonderful to have a youngster around again. Hertha's off early every day to the hospital and comes back late; such long hours. She's found his mother a little job there on two afternoons. It's such a good life that she feels guilty sometimes. Rolf is well, the apartment is still untouched. Perhaps they'll be lucky, and it will survive. She tries not to think of the past. *You know what I mean*, she says, *but of course, when I think of you, Ilse is always there, too.*

The package contains a small jeweller's box – Lotte's engagement ring. The accompanying letter is a different kettle of fish entirely from his mother's:

Murville,

I will not address you by your rank; you are not worthy of it. Your outrageous conduct in my office has been exceeded only by your behaviour towards my daughter, which has been utterly despicable. I would dearly love to drag you through the courts to seek restitution for the injury you have inflicted but Lotte has begged me not to. She says she cannot face the uproar. She needs to preserve her strength for her teaching, which is vital for the nation, helping to bring to the next generation the principles and ideals of National Socialism. It is a tribute to her courage and resolve that she has continued to work without cease since the day of your infamous rejection. She is returning your trinket, for which of course she has no further use. It has tainted the atmosphere of our home long enough.

Your face is everywhere we look. If people knew what we know, you would not receive such acclaim. I despise you and look forward eagerly to news of your demise.

Josef Hofmann, Doctor.

No best wishes? The joke, a mental reflex, fails to numb the appalling shock he feels at having generated such hatred. It's the most unpleasant letter he's ever received, but then, could he have expected anything less? Neither Hofmann nor Lotte have any conception of the revulsion they've caused in him. Does everyone in the family think the same way? Anna, the bright, hard-working medical student sister, who often asked him questions about the physical effects of war flying? Frau Hofmann, with the look and air of a film star, such a good advert for Lotte's more mature years to come, who always seemed to be flirting with him but was ever kind and welcoming? Are they all Nazi adherents, avid supporters of the work of the head of the family, the habitue of death camps: Hofmann, the monster who applauds experiments on twins?

He resists the urge to tear the letter up. He might want to stuff it down Hofmann's throat sometime. He puts it back in the envelope. The ring he doesn't want. He couldn't ever give it to anyone else. He puts it in his pocket. There are diamonds on it. He'll keep it for a rainy day, along with his second-best Knight's Cross with Diamonds. Quite a nest egg he's building up.

He's gazing at the photograph of Gerda and his daughter Ilse when Scholz knocks and comes in with a cable. He's been awarded the Combat Clasp for Fighters in Gold with Diamonds. The Führer wants him at the *Wolfschanze*. It's happened. More diamonds!

Eventually, he reads the accompanying memo. He's currently the leading destroyer of heavy bombers with twenty confirmed victories. Ten men fly in each B17. Allowing for some who bale out, he must have killed at least a hundred Americans.

He has four days to think the assassination through.

Still a twinge in his ankle but he forgets it when he spots the two Mustangs chasing a 190 just above the fields.

'Indians! Ten o'clock low.'

'Victor, victor,' he hears from Flo.

The 190 is trailing smoke. It's a distant shot but he takes it. He's doing five fifty after his dive and the recoil from the guns slows him considerably. Hits sparkle around the Ami's cockpit. The Mustang turns on its back and ploughs into the ground. The 190 is climbing, the smoke is thicker and blacker now. The second Mustang is turning to the right and suddenly gushes smoke from the engine. The nose goes down and the Ami heads for the ground to belly land.

'Saw it, Flo! Good shooting!' he calls, and there's a tearing sound and an immediate great pain in his face, in his left eye. Almost blind, he breaks right and climbs. He puts a hand to his temple and cheek. His glove is covered in blood when he takes it away.

'I'm hit. Going home. Am I clear?'

'Yes,' Flo calls through the crackle. 'Mustang. It's gone. Came from nowhere. Didn't see it. No visible damage.'

'I can't see with my left eye.'

They get back to the field. Flo flies alongside and metre by metre talks him onto the ground. They pull him out. Walk him away from the Gustav. In the medical room the doc swabs his face down and then sucks air in between his teeth.

'Bad?' Jochen says.

'Could be better. Does it hurt?'

'Like a bastard. Feels like I've got a lump of wood in my eye.'

'Not wood. Metal.'

Jochen imagines life solely on the ground. If he can't see, he can't fly.

The Doc turns away and rummages for something.

'I expect this will hurt but I can't do anything about that. Metal splinter. I've got a magnet here. I hope I can get it out the way it went in. Look to the right. And don't move. Ready?'

He can't describe the pain. It's bad but afterwards he won't think about it. It's gone, he hopes.

'Good,' the doc says. 'Finished.' He swabs all around Jochen's eye again and puts a pad over it. 'Hold that there.' He winds a bandage round his head and over his eye.

'Can I have a drink?'

'You should. Me too.' The Doc takes his arm and walks him out.

He lies in bed that evening and hugs the pain to himself, but he's in his office the next day, pain not quite so bad. Two days later the bandage comes off in a darkened room. He sees blurs. The Doc gives him an eye patch.

'Snap,' he says to Scholz. The guys call them the pirate twins.

Schaefer leads the *gruppe*. Flo is missing after they come across Mustangs.

He can't remember when he last played or put a record on. His mood is too low to contemplate it. They'll all be dead soon. Leningrad's gone. All those guys out there, killed or captured. Germany will fall. The music hall comic is tossing everyone into the mincer. Not just the young men but everyone left at home in the cities, too. They're dying under the bombs day and night, while all the clown does is think of new awards to give to the likes of Jochen in absurd little ceremonies.

With his eye as it is, he probably won't die in the air now. The only way he'll be able to affect events will be with that Beretta. And his mother?

Five other officers join him on the regular transport from Rangsdorf to Rastenburg: three Luftwaffe guys for Oak Leaves and Swords, a U-boat captain for the same and a tank commander for a simple Knight's Cross. The tank guy doesn't know what it is he's done to get it. He just shoots up Commie tanks every day, he says. The others are all pleased with the couple of days free of duties and ready to start drinking as soon as possible. Jochen's eye hurts much less now but he follows orders and keeps the patch on. An ordinary staff car meets them, not Fatty's limousine. Jochen's heard rumours that the fat man is out of favour, owing to his failure to stop the bombing. As they're about to leave, a car hurtles up from the direction of the *Wolfschanze*. The passengers hurry across the tarmac to another waiting Junkers. One of them has a black eye patch identical to his. A Wehrmacht *Oberst*. Only one arm, as well. He's done his bit! And then Jochen forgets him.

The Beretta sits over his heart in an inside tunic pocket. It presses against him as the car throws him around on bends. If they find it and he hasn't disclosed it, the trouble will start. He'll have to claim forgetfulness and give them his story with an air of innocence. But if he gets inside with it undetected? He still doesn't know. He imagines his mother being slapped around. Beaten to the floor. Guillotined.

The others natter away. The U-boat captain sits next to the driver and leans over the back of the seat to join in. He laughs often. Jochen doesn't take part. He stares out of the window. Fields give way to dark, oppressive ranks of fir trees that crowd the road, throw it into shadow. They probably all think he's a stuck-up bastard, so young, with the Diamonds at his throat, too good to talk to the likes of them.

What result does he want from shooting Hitler? The chance for a great victory directed by someone who might actually manage it? Who could? Rommel or someone like him? Is it even possible to defeat the Yanks? With all their factories working? Fortresses and Mustangs lined up wing tip to wing tip? And the Russians? The British? A negotiated peace, then? But why would the Allies do that? They're winning. The Luftwaffe will be gone soon. Those super weapons he's heard rumours of? They'll be too late, like the 262. A surrender? To stop the killing? To keep some Germans alive? Children at least, like Lilo's baby, Andreas. And what would happen with Hitler gone? Who would take over? Unless there was a plan, probably Goering and Himmler. Then what? Goering apparently hates Himmler's guts. It's probably mutual. One of them would get rid of the other. While the country goes down the toilet.

He should have some others behind him to take advantage of the situation. He's got no one. He'll just be carrying out zu Sayn-Wittgenstein's deathbed wish. Get rid of the guttersnipe. Is that a good enough justification? Cause some chaos, or rather greater chaos, and let what happens happen. With all this thinking, is he trying to justify doing nothing? Is he finding reasons for not going through with it just to protect his mother from her fate? Should there even be a victory? Would it be right? Or a peace, even? What about those camps? All those poor devils! What about Hofmann and Mengele? And the others who must be aiding and abetting them? If Germany won, they'd all just carry on.

They pull up at the gate and are let through the outer ring of fencing. Two more rings of fencing to go. The driver's just pulling away when an SS *leutnant* dashes out of a hut and in front of the car. He raises a hand to stop them.

'What's up?' the U-boat captain says through his window. The *leutnant* doesn't answer but signals the driver to pull off the road and park. He goes back into the hut.

Jochen passes his cigarettes around as they get out to stretch their legs.

'Feeling better?' the U-boat captain says to Jochen.

'It's no good,' the tank guy says, 'I can't wait any longer.' He disappears behind the hut, opening his flies as he goes. One of the Luftwaffe officers follows him. They're a long time gone.

'When's the wedding?' the U-boat captain calls as they stride back.

The tank guy calls them into a huddle. 'There was a window open. It's uproar in there. They're talking about what to do. There's been an explosion.'

'Where?' the captain says.

'Down there!' The tank guy points down the road to where Jochen knows the *Wolfschanze* lies. His heart leaps.

'I doubt we'll be meeting our leader today,' the Luftwaffe officer says.

'You mean, he was in the explosion?' Jochen can hardly dare to hope.

'I didn't hear anyone say that, but it sounds like much too big a kerfuffle for anyone to be presenting awards any time soon.'

Jochen sees eyes dart around the group. They stay silent. No one wants to speak. The only possible public comment would be a prayer for the Führer's safety, but no one utters a word.

He lights another cigarette and wanders off towards the fence. He stares at the dark firs two hundred metres away. Has he been saved from his own folly? Has his mother been rescued by providence? Has the country been rescued? It must have been a bomb. Who did it? How he hopes it got him! Zu Sayn-Wittgenstein will be dancing with glee on a heavenly cloud.

Behind him on the road he hears a *kübelwagen* arrive at high speed and pull up with screeching brakes. A shouting man gets out. Jochen drops his cigarette and turns to see what's going on. The noisy man, a *Hauptmann* of SS, sees him, draws his pistol and runs at him. Three of his men follow him.

'You're under arrest! Put your hands up!'

Jochen laughs but with a highly excited SS guy waving a gun in his face he obeys. He sees his companions approaching.

'What the fuck's going on?' the U-boat captain says.

'Not your business. Shut up!'

'Don't talk to me like that, pipsqueak!'

The SS *Hauptmann* takes control. 'That's it, you're all under arrest.'

The troopers have their machine pistols trained on them.

'You're going to be very sorry about this!' the captain says.

'Over there, against the hut.'

What is this? A summary execution?

'I'm not standing up against any walls,' the tank guy says.

'Give me your pistol,' the SS *Hauptmann* says, still pointing his gun at Jochen.

Jochen hands it over and the *Hauptmann* passes it to one of his troopers.

'What is it you think I've done?'

'The eye patch. It gives you away. Now get over there against that wall.' He pokes Jochen with his pistol. The barrel digging into his chest irritates Jochen. It's like a push from someone in the playground. He wants to push back. He stands his ground.

'Move!'

'I'm damned if I will.'

'I'll have to shoot.'

Jochen laughs. He still has his hands in the air. He lowers them.

'Get your hands up!' He pokes Jochen again and the snout of the pistol presses against the Beretta inside Jochen's tunic.

'What's this?' The *Hauptmann* pulls opens a button, slides his hand inside and pulls out the Beretta.

'Hauptmann!' the captain shouts. 'That's enough! Stop acting like a hysterical girl and explain yourself!'

'I don't have to explain to you. I'm SS.'

The captain draws his own pistol. 'Explain, sonny, or

you'll be the one with a bullet in your gut.'

The tank guy and the other Luftwaffe officers also now have pistols in their hands.

The *Hauptmann* looks at the guns pointing at him. 'An officer wearing an eye patch left a briefcase in the Führer's conference room,' he says. 'It contained a bomb, which went off. My orders are to find the officer and detain him.'

'Is the Führer safe?'

'I don't know.'

The tank guy disappears into the hut. The captain shakes his head.

'Is everyone in the SS as stupid as you? Look—' the captain begins, but the SS *leutnant* rushes out of the hut and interrupts.

'Sir! These officers have just arrived. I told them to wait while it was decided how we should proceed.'

'There,' the captain says, 'all explained.'

The tank guy emerges from the hut and comes over. 'Thanks to our comrade, I imagine. This officer has been in our company for many hours since we gathered in Berlin for our flight here. And anyway, you must be the only person in Germany who doesn't recognise him.'

The *Hauptmann* looks at the tank guy and the captain, and at Jochen. He puts his gun away.

'I'll have my weapons back now and an apology,' Jochen says.

The *Hauptmann* jerks his head at the trooper holding Jochen's Walther pistol. He hands it back and Jochen holsters it. Jochen holds his hand out for the Beretta.

'What's this for?' the *Hauptmann* says. 'Hidden away like that.'

'Mind your own business.'

'Why are you bringing a concealed weapon to the Führer's HQ?'

'Not concealed, in my pocket.'

'All the same,' the SS man says as he passes it over.

'I'm not answering your questions. Now apologise.'

'I won't apologise for doing my job.'

Jochen turns his back on the SS man and walks to the fence. The sun is warm on his face. The shadow of those trees doesn't quite reach him. He hears a slight breeze moving through the tops of them but there are no birds singing here. He feels agitated. He hopes Hitler is dead. He lights a cigarette. The flame of the zippo flickers. Is his hand shaking?

An officer with an eye patch; the one-armed guy hurrying to the Junkers. He was with people, were they part of a plot? He hopes they've got generals attached to it; the guy was only an *Oberst*. Jochen won't be shooting anyone today. They'll probably be out of here soon.

He hears a footstep and turns. The U-boat captain.

'Thank you for all that,' Jochen says.

'I hate those bastards,' the captain says. 'They tried to put them on our boats to report back on us.'

'Really?'

The captain nods. 'What's that gun for anyway?'

'Insurance, in case I come down on the other side.'

'Oh. You weren't planning to shoot him then?'

8

Raindrop Prelude

'How long have you got to keep it on?'

He's lying on the grass in the sun, Hertha's sitting on the swing that hangs from a bough of the massive oak to one side of the drive. He looks up at her and shades his good eye with his hand.

'Another week, the doc said.'

'Can you take it off at night?'

'To sleep. If the room's dark.'

She's got the grey slacks on she was wearing that winter morning he turned up here to ask if his mother could come to stay. No jumper though. A pink blouse instead. Her hair is dragged off her face and tied back. He's wearing his desert issue khaki trousers and one of Lilo's husband's white shirts. They don't smile. They know each other well enough not to have to.

'Does it hurt?'

'Not really. Stings a bit.'

'Will you have to stop flying?'

'No idea.'

'Will you mind if you have to?'

'Probably. It's been my life.'

'It looks very dashing.'

'Like a pirate?'

She laughs and stands up from the swing. 'I have to go and change. Your mother will be home with the bike soon.'

They walk across the grass to the house and then round the side to the kitchen door. They climb the stairs together, but Hertha leaves him to go to her room to put on her uniform for the hospital and he goes up another flight to his room under the eaves.

He lies on the bed. He's been at the house for five hours. Jonny Beck told him to go on leave until he knew something about his eye. There's no one for him to see in Berlin, really, so he hitched a ride in a plane to Neunerstadt and knocked on the door, bag in hand.

Actually, he'll be devastated if he can't fly. Devastated but alive. Probably. Unless something else happens. He's had his nine English lives now. Perhaps it's a good time to put away his wings.

The house is silent. No baby noises; Andreas must be napping. The window hangs open but there's no breeze to relieve the temperature up here under the roof. The comedian survived the bomb. National thanksgiving on the wireless, nationwide relief and anger. Beck was apoplectic but many in the *gruppe* were silent. The one-armed man with the eye patch was from a 'good' family, as zu Sayn-Wittgenstein would have said. Oberst Claus Von Stauffenberg. Shot the same day along with others. It must have been a real plot to have organised a bomb and bring it in. Who will ever get near Hitler now? He hears a faint bicycle bell from the drive below and he's coming down the stairs as his mother hurries out of the kitchen, just back from the hospital and just told that he's here.

'Jochen!' She runs to him and hugs him. 'Why didn't you say you were coming? They told me about your poor eye. How is it? Does it hurt badly? How did it happen? Will you have to stop flying? I so hope you do. How long are you staying? Have you eaten? You're probably starving. You look so thin as usual.'

Later, they sit on a bench under the roses in the garden behind the house. Everybody else has left them alone to talk.

'I have something to tell you.'

'You've made it up with Lotte.'

'Certainly not.'

'What then?'

'I've heard from Gerda.'

'From Sweden?'

He nods.

'Is she well?'

'Yes. She's working for a family. They're very kind, she says. It's a good country, with good people.'

'I'm glad. She's a nice girl.'

He puts his hand in his pocket.

'She sent a photo.'

He passes it to her. His mother looks at it and then at

Jochen. She turns it over and reads the name. She gasps and puts a hand to her mouth. 'She's yours.'

'Yes, Mother. And yours. Your granddaughter. Gerda says it was the only name she could choose.'

His mother pulls out a handkerchief and wipes her eyes. She studies the photograph. 'Your eyes. She has them.'

'Yes?'

'Definitely.' She's silent for a moment, gazing at the photograph. 'It must be difficult for her. Alone. With a baby. Awkward, too.'

'She's told everyone she's my wife.'

'Has she? Is that why you couldn't marry Lotte? Jochen!'

'No! I told you. Lotte is the reason I couldn't marry Lotte.' He puts a hand in his pocket. 'Here, read Gerda's letter.'

'It's an honourable letter,' she says when she passes it back. 'Do you mind her lies?'

'What else could she do?'

'Are you going to marry her? Didn't I hear of a way that soldiers at the front can marry their girls back home?'

'I don't think it works in my situation. I'm in Germany, she's abroad and she's Jewish. A bit difficult to fill in a form with all the details.'

'What will you do?'

'I don't know what I can do. Send her money, I suppose.'

'How?'

'I think I have a way.'

His mother breathes out heavily.

'I'm sorry this was such a shock.'

She manages a smile.

'But,' he says, 'if anything happens to me, will you get in touch with her? Get to know Ilse. Help them.'

'But she'll still be Jewish, Jochen. It'd be almost impossible. The law. How could I? I couldn't even go there, could I?'

'We aren't going to win, Mother. All these laws will be swept away. Quite soon.'

'Is that what you think?'

'We're being overwhelmed. Our armies are retreating everywhere.'

'Again! How terrible!'

'More terrible to have these monsters remain in power.'

'Shhh!'

'No one can hear. And don't they all agree?'

'Don't test them, Jochen. You never really know what anyone thinks.'

'Will you get in touch with Gerda though, if I'm not here?'

She takes his hands. 'Of course, darling. I'll do everything in my power to help them.'

'And be family to them?'

'As much as I can be.'

That night the heat wakes him up and he can't get to sleep again. He lies in the dark but finally gets up, opens the curtains and stands at the window in just his shorts as the air comes in onto his face, his chest. There's a moon. It throws a huge shadow from the oak across the silvery grass. From the air the pale gravel drive must be like an arrow pointing at the house. A wonderful target for someone flying home low with ammunition left.

He lies down again. Memories! So many he's flown with in the *Geschwader* who've died. He counts them off on his fingers. He's on the fourth round of his fingers, he thinks, thirty plus, when he gives up. He keeps forgetting where he's got to and anyway, he returns again and again to Franz, still in his Friedrich, in a hole four or five metres deep in the desert.

When Jochen told him he was going to marry Lotte, how Franz laughed! Jochen, the cynical, never-marry fighter pilot. And each agreed to be the other's best man! What a waste. And how much he still misses him. He sits up and lights a cigarette.

The door opens and closes.

'Jochen.'

'Hertha. Still in your uniform.'

'I was with Lilo. Then I fell asleep. She's not very good at night. She lies there imagining Stalingrad and Karl dying in a prison camp and a lifetime alone. Can we talk a while?'

'Sure.' He puts his cigarette out and slides over on the bed.

They lie side by side. She asks about Lotte, and he tells her about their bust up and his interview with Dr Hofmann.

'Can that be true? I've heard her father spoken of. He's distinguished in his field. Looked up to. Did he just come out with it?'

'I asked about his work.'

'And Lotte didn't mind?'

'I think she's proud of him.'

She's silent for a while. He leaves her with her thoughts but she's asleep, he realises. Her head has turned towards him. He looks at her face in the moonlight and closes his eyes.

He wakes when Hertha moves and disturbs the arm he's thrown across her in his sleep. Sunlight is streaming into the room and onto their faces. She smiles at him, leaves the bed and creeps out.

To earn his keep he chops wood outside the kitchen door. It's another hot day, but if they want to cook they need the stove alight. After lunch, dappled by sun and leaves, he falls asleep in a hammock strung between apple trees.

He feels guilty lazing around and tells his mother.

'You're wounded,' she says. 'Don't feel guilty. This is your task at the moment. Get well. It was an order, wasn't it?'

He shuts the door on himself and plays for three hours. It's the most practice he's managed in a long time. It becomes clear to him how rusty he is. After getting his fingers moving, he plays scales and then practises a piece that's new to him: Chopin's *Raindrop Prelude*. The piece and the playing cheer him. When he looks round, he sees Hertha on one of the window seats. Her back is against the return of the wall and her bare feet flat on the seat, raising her knees. Below her skirt her calf has an appealing curve to it.

'Don't stop.' Her eyes are closed, and she doesn't turn her head to him.

'I didn't realise you were here.'

'I crept in. Carry on. The whole house is listening.'

He plays the piece again without stopping.

'Can't you tell them your eye is permanently damaged?'

'They'll test it.'

'You can fake it.'

'Hertha!'

'Oh, sorry! German officer! Haven't you done enough? All your decorations?'

'What would I do? Tour the country playing Chopin to houses full of women?'

She comes to his room again. It's still hot. The moon pours through the window.

'Hertha!' he says as she sits on the bed.

'What? Lotte's gone, isn't she? For good.'

'Yes, but...'

The moon is on her face as she looks down at him. A smile of comprehension appears. 'Oh, I see. There's someone else. Fast work, Jochen.'

'There was always someone else, Hertha.'

'It didn't matter before.'

'Things have changed.'

'Mystery man.'

Can he tell her about Gerda? Of course, he can't.

'I'm sorry to sound mysterious.'

'Someone's wife? Magda Goebbels?'

'No one's wife.'

She stares down at him still. 'Fine. OK.'

'Stay friends?'

She shrugs and stands and leaves silently.

He lights a cigarette, lays the ashtray on his chest. Should he have put his arm around her? No. Terrible idea. So, is he going to be faithful now? To Gerda? Mother of his daughter. He hasn't considered that at all, really. It happened out of the blue just now with Hertha. Or was he just being kind? Imagining that perhaps she wanted to invest more in him than he can offer back?

After a month, he thinks his eye is back to normal. He pushes to go back to his *gruppe*. Schaefer's still there, doing well, apart from the constant loss of green pilots.

'Obey orders,' Jonny says when Jochen rings to persuade him to agitate to get him back, and, 'I had to tell that Gestapo guy to fuck off again. He's quite persistent. Seems sure you're a murderer. I told him you only murder Americans.'

They assign him to Galland's staff and give him half an office in Berlin. He stays with Rolf. The apartment is still untouched. The club has gone in a pile of rubble, though, and he can't find Otto. He prays he isn't underneath it.

His job is to tour fighter bases, talk to the guys, check on morale, discuss tactics, report back. He travels as adjutant to his old boss, Winter, who's actually one of Galland's long term pals from Condor Legion days in Spain, fighting Commies even back then in the thirties. Winter's normal, of course; no Nazi bullshit. They travel in armed Gustavs and he flies as wing-man in case Ami fighters spot them. It's a comfortable job but Jochen wonders what the point of it is. Unit commanders should be doing all this without superiors visiting and asking questions. The guilt he feels at not being with his *gruppe* is always there.

Rommel's in hospital, he hears. Badly injured in a strafing attack. That will make life easier for the invaders. Not that they seem to need any help.

At one field they visit there's a hangar full of captured Allied aircraft to test against German types. He has a wonderful day in the air. He goes straight to the Spitfire, looking strange with black crosses. It's a joy but then he puts the nose straight down and the engine cuts out. He loves everything about the Mustang, though. Good view. And powerful. The dive! Landing is easy, too, with the very wide undercarriage. Oh, for a Mustang! Behind him, the fuselage is really a giant fuel tank, the secret of the Mustang's huge range.

They visit the Eastern Front. The units they go to aren't as demoralised as those flying in the West, although they're just as outnumbered. The Russian pilots aren't as proficient as the Amis and the British, and the units lose their new pilots slightly less regularly.

With two days free in Berlin, he sets out to find Otto. Perhaps he's playing somewhere else now. He tries all the clubs he can think of, talks to the musicians. One says he believes Otto's still around. Another says Otto was talking of going to his brother's place on the coast. He plays once or twice but it's not the same without Otto.

He goes to the area Otto lived in and wanders about. The address is gone. Another heap of rubble. He asks and asks and when the name clearly means nothing, describes Otto.

'I've seen him,' one or two say, but can't remember exactly when or where.

Galland presents him with the Gold Combat Clasp that Hitler couldn't on the day of the bomb. They eat at the Adlon, patched up from its damage and still crowded with staff officers and their shining girls. Galland's Baroness has gone west into the country with her children.

He drinks brandy at home with Rolf, who looks haggard. The apartment isn't too much of a mess. The next morning, Rolf's left for the office and Jochen's drinking acorn coffee in the kitchen when the bell rings. It's Otto.

'I heard you were looking for me,' he says. Jochen wants to hug him, but they shake hands, both grinning. They go inside and sit in the kitchen. Jochen pours coffee.

'What's this?' Jochen flicks Otto's arm with the back of his fingers.

'Dr Goebbels' latest plan for me.'

Otto has an arm band round the left sleeve of his dark grey suit jacket: *Deutscher Volkssturm Wehrmacht* in silver on black.

'It's my third day. I'm a *feldwebel*. I have to drill a bunch of fourteen-year-old kids in an hour's time.'

'What's the *Volkssturm* supposed to do?'

'Repel the Red Army when they get here. Goebbels wants us to show our crack troops how to do what millions of them haven't managed.'

'What with?'

'We've got some broom handles and a couple of the lads brought shovels along.'

'God!'

'I've heard rumours of grenades and old rifles coming our way though. That's worse. These kids of mine will think they can fight if they get a gun. And they'll expect me to stay there and die with them.'

'I'm sorry they've got hold of you.'

'Not as sorry as me. I should have gone to the coast while I had the chance.'

'Listen.' Jochen tells Otto all his news.

'You do live an exciting life. Congratulations. It's not the best time to become a father, though.'

Jochen wants him to get some money to Uwe for Gerda, but Otto is doubtful about it.

'If you post it, it'll get stolen and if you send it to be signed for, it gets too noticeable. There'd be a record. And sending currency to Sweden? Bound to be illegal. They'd be down on you like a ton of bricks. I expect Uwe could find a Swedish captain or crewman who'd help you out if you got the money to him. But who would want to exchange marks in Sweden?'

Otto gives Jochen his new address. 'It's a tiny back room in a half-derelict building. I share it with a cat who keeps the rats at bay, but the landlady gives me a bowl of soup most evenings.'

Jochen walks him down the stairs and sees him out, watches him make his way along the street under the limes still clinging to their colour, though the colour will change soon and the leaves will fall before long. Old men, too ancient or unfit for the army, and boys, that's Germany's last line of defence. And girls. He went past a flak battery earlier, where a group in League of German Girls' uniforms were stacking shells.

Winter tells him Rommel has died of his injuries. Jochen falls silent as he takes in the news. They might as well surrender now. Poor devil. He remembers a jovial night in the desert: brandy and toasts and Jonny Beck leaving as they grew irreverent about the Führer.

Later, they're deciding their itinerary for the week when there's a knock and a corporal enters with a message. Winter hands it over to Jochen and picks up the phone.

'Get me General Galland.' He talks and listens for three or four minutes then puts the phone down. 'He says get down there and investigate. He'll tell Goering. Fatty'll be livid.'

They fly down to Moetzlich, an airfield near Halle, not far from Weimar. There was an air raid there a couple of days before. Fortresses bombed the underground factory that makes aircraft components for Siebel. They have to report on the damage. At least, that's the official reason for their trip here. They borrow a *kübelwagen* and drive to the factory.

Massive craters in the fields all around, but after a day clearing rubble to restore access, it seems production is up and running again. Winter asks questions, Jochen writes the answers down in a foolscap notebook. Workers wearing striped uniforms emerge from the hillside at intervals. They blink in the sunlight and load coils and sheets of metal from covered stores into trucks that they trundle along rails into the cave the factory occupies. The men are gaunt and slow moving, shaven-headed, grey-faced, exhausted-looking. Some glance at him but then look away quickly, concentrating on their task again.

'What are they paid?' Jochen asks the manager they're talking to, a portly, grey-haired man in a brown overall coat.

He laughs. 'They're Poles and Czechs.'

'And?'

The man laughs again. 'We pay the SS four marks a day per worker.'

'Murville,' Winter says, 'our report isn't on the work force. Thank you, then,' he says to the manager, 'we'll be on our way. Buchenwald?'

'That way.' The man waves an arm. 'You'll probably smell it before you see it.'

Back in the *kübelwagen*, Jochen takes a turn to the left and they're soon going down a fine country road, glowing green pasture on each side, cows grazing; the odd cart pulled by an ox, driven by a woman walking at the ox's head; a timber church to the right standing out against a brilliant white cloud on the horizon; on a low hill, a copse of stick-like birches, their leaves nearly gone; the light from the weak sun bringing charm to the whole panorama. A scene Goethe would have surely appreciated when he wandered around here.

'So, they're slaves then, those guys, is that it?' Jochen says.

'In effect. They must be.'

'And we're fighting for that? That's what we all have to die for?'

'There's no answer to that for us, is there? And slow down.'

The road they begin to climb has beeches on each side. A beautiful wood of beeches. They glance at each other as they detect the smell, foul and difficult to identify. The trees open and give way to the camp. There's a brick gatehouse with a pyramidal roof. Barbed wire fences stretch away on each flank. Jochen pulls up at the gate. Worked into the metal of the gate is the motto: *Jedem Das Seine*. Through the gate he sees thin men shuffling around in those striped uniforms.

'We need to speak to a senior officer here,' Winter says when a guard emerges. The guard swings the gate open and Jochen drives through. He parks off the road, which continues through the camp.

'What the fuck does that mean on the gate, "to each his own"?'

'Just keep quiet, Murville. Let me do the talking. You won't achieve anything by losing your rag. This is what we've really flown down here for, remember.'

A *Hauptmann* of the SS marches up and salutes. 'Good day, sir. What can we do for you?' He nods at Jochen.

'We'd like to see your roll of detainees and have a look around. We heard a rumour that there are allied airmen here, which, of course, is against all regulations since everyone knows that captured airmen are the responsibility of the Luftwaffe.' Winter smiles. 'There must have been an administrative error somewhere.'

'I don't know where you can have heard that, sir...'

Jochen wanders off and hears no more. There are two

wire fences, and he walks beside the inner one. There's a small parade area at the centre of the camp with huts situated around it, a lot of huts. They've been here some time. The wood has weathered to grey. He walks on. He's following orders. Winter didn't know how they'd be received so he told Jochen to make sure he got a good look around at once before things got difficult, as he thought they might.

He fights the urge to gag at the smell. What is it? Shit, of course, but more than that. Dead bodies? He saw and smelled a good few in France in 1940. How can there be rotting bodies left above ground in a place this size? There'd be awful problems with disease.

A man in stripes shuffles past. He averts his eyes when he sees Jochen looking at him. The man disappears between two huts. A nearby hut door hangs open. Jochen sees bunks closely packed inside, ranging into the darkness, no inmates in evidence. He turns away from the stench that reaches him, bodies and filth this time. He goes past more huts.

There's nobody around. Are they all working somewhere? Movement catches his eye. Two men in the usual stripes carry another out of a hut. One has his hands under the armpits, the other has the knees. The man they're carrying is desperately thin. They lay him down on a hand cart near the hut. His head flops to one side. A corpse. The men go back into the hut without making a sound. Are they going to bring out another? He looks from left to right as he walks. All the huts look the same. He's in a nightmare, doomed to confront horror at each turn.

He stops and looks back. The men emerge with another corpse hanging between them and lay it next to the first on the cart. The huts throw shadows in the autumn sun but there's no joy in the sunlight that falls on the roofs. He looks up. There are no birds in view and no sounds of birds to be heard. No sounds at all, in fact.

He walks on. He's looking for Allied airman, but where are they? Perhaps he should call out but before he can, he hears a shout himself.

'Hauptmann Murville! Jochen!'

He swings about. There's a barefoot man in stripes limping as he hurries towards him.

'Jochen!'

Who can it be? Some poor devil from Berlin? It's a Berlin accent. Some Jew he knew and liked? From school? Too young for Herr Walter. Dark hair. He stares hard at the face. Thin, dirty, bearded. But that nose. The eyes. There was no beard before. It can't be.

'Sam Levine?'

'The one and only. I saw you go by. Jesus! This is some kind of miracle! Listen! You've got to get us out of here before we all die. There's two guys gone already. There are a lot of us here and we shouldn't be.'

'We know, Sam, we'll get you out. We got a message. You look terrible.'

'I expect so.'

'Where are your shoes?'

'Confiscated. We refused to work.'

'We need to talk to my boss,' Jochen says. 'He's at the gatehouse. Where are the others?'

Levine turns, puts two fingers in his mouth and whistles. Figures come round the corner of a hut, become a crowd. They're all in stripes. Levine beckons them with a wave of his arm. There's a command. The men stop and rapidly form three ranks. Another command and the troop that's formed turns to the right and starts to march towards Jochen.

'Marching!' Jochen says.

'The Old Man insists on it.'

Winter is coming across the parade ground followed by the SS *Hauptmann* and half a dozen troopers.

'This place, Jochen!' Levine says. 'They work these other poor bastards to death, the food is diabolical. They're nearly all Jews. Like me.'

The marching troop wheels right and, on command, halts. As far as Jochen can see, none of them have shoes. A tall man wearing stripes moves from the head of the column to stand before the front rank. His face is badly bruised. Jochen salutes. At attention, the man says in English, 'Squadron Leader Lamason. In command here.'

Levine translates.

Also still at attention, Jochen says, 'Hauptmann Murville. Please have your men stand at ease, Squadron Leader.'

Levine translates and the order is given. Levine continues to translate for them. Jochen doesn't feel confident enough of his English here to speak directly.

'What happened to your face, Squadron Leader?'

'Your colleagues who operate this place weren't pleased when I told them we refused to work.'

'Do any of you have shoes?'

'None. Punishment.'

Jochen is deeply shocked.

Winter arrives. He turns to the *Hauptmann*. 'Get these men some shoes immediately.'

'They're under punishment, sir. They refuse to work.'

'Of course, they do. They're officers and prisoners of war. They're not obliged to work and shouldn't be told to.'

'It's the commandant's order, sir.'

'I'll talk to him on his return from his visit. In the meantime, shoes! At once!'

The *Hauptmann* sends two troopers scurrying off. Winter turns to Lamason and salutes him. Lamason comes to attention. Jochen introduces them. He looks around. What a desperate, bare and terrifying place this is.

'We must take a roll of everyone here. Murville,' Winter says. 'Get everyone's name, rank and number.'

Lamason gives the order to open ranks and then moves with Jochen down the lines, stopping at each man. Lamason impresses Jochen by giving him just about every name and nationality himself; British, Canadian, Australian, American, New Zealander, Jamaican. Levine helps with spellings when necessary. Winter remains behind and engages the *Hauptmann* in a conversation that the *Hauptmann* would clearly rather not be having. Jochen has filled five pages before he finishes. Some men are in the hospital. He can't imagine what that will be like in this place. He adds their names and those of the two dead men.

Lamason leads them off a good distance from his men. He tells Levine not to join them. He clearly wants a private conversation. He speaks slowly to Jochen in English.

'Please help us very soon. The Russians in this camp, the Communists, know everything. They got the message out for us. They say we will be executed in a few days.'

'Executed?' Jochen is stunned. 'Killed?'

'Shot. On the 26th of October.'

'Why?'

'We are spies and terror flyers, they say.'

Jochen translates.

'Executed?' Winter says in a loud voice.

'Don't shout,' Lamason says, 'I haven't told my men yet.'

'We'll start on this at once, squadron leader.' Winter signals to the *Hauptmann*. 'Come with me. I want a telephone line to Berlin now.'

Jochen goes over to Levine and puts out his hand. Levine shakes it.

'He's going to call Goering.'

'Thanks, buddy.'

Jochen must speak but what to say? This is what the Reich is. This place. This place of horror where men are worked to death and bodies are loaded onto handcarts to go... where? A pit? A fire? He fears he might weep. The shame! To stand before an enemy and feel like this!

'I apologise, Sam,' he says after a moment. 'I didn't think anything like this could happen.'

Levine looks into his eyes, 'You should have, Jochen. It's why we're fighting you.'

9

The Tempest

Galland wants to gather up every unit they've got. Three thousand fighters to attack a big raid. He wants to destroy four or five hundred heavy Ami bombers in one go. That will stop them in their tracks, he hopes. It will mean training up the new guys and not attacking raids piecemeal while they do so. It might work. Higher up seems to agree. Not Goering, he's in bad odour and doesn't see Hitler. The last thing he seems to have achieved, apparently by shouting and screaming at Himmler, is to get those Allied airmen out of Buchenwald, the beech forest, and into Stalag Luft III.

'I have an apology to make,' Winter said as Jochen drove them away from the camp that day. 'They are slaves in that factory, and I didn't believe you in the desert when you told us about the officers you heard talking about the plans for the Jews. You were right and that place we've just left… if I hadn't seen it, I wouldn't believe it existed. But what we can do about it, I have no idea. I know I'll never forget it.'

Jochen can't forget it, either. If he's got no immediate task to hand, it's there, front and centre: the smell, the wraiths carrying the dead men from the huts, the happy, confident SS *Hauptmann* and the guards unbothered and carefree going about their business.

He's supposed to be putting together a report on a recent visit to a unit based in France, but what's the point? It'll get sent upstairs and stuck in a filing cabinet. He's lost all faith in his superiors. Goering's chief of staff, General Kreipe, has been banned from Hitler's HQ for arguing with him, and a General Christian, whom Jochen's never heard of, is doing the talking and making decisions, aided by Herbert Buchs. Just a major! It's very dispiriting to learn how things are actually decided. Oh, to be back leading his *gruppe*, knowing nothing of all this incompetence. And Rommel didn't die of injuries, he was ordered to take poison. That's the rumour. For being part of the bomb plot. If only it had succeeded! Stauffenberg and his friends will be German heroes in a few years' time.

An orderly enters. 'Downstairs has just called up, sir. There's a Gestapo man in the lobby who wants to talk to you.'

'Name?'

'Kriminal kommissar Heinecke, sir.'

Jesus Christ! 'Thanks.'

Out of the back door? No, get it over with. He grabs his cap.

'Tell Oberst Winter where I've gone, will you?'

Heinecke is sitting on a wooden bench against the wall with his hat on his lap. The good suit, the dark, brilliantined, brushed-back hair. As Jochen crosses the marble floor, footsteps echoing in the huge space, Heinecke stands.

'Jochen.'

'Heinecke.'

'I thought we were on first name terms.'

'We might have been. Before you told my boss I murdered your brother.'

'He may have jumped to conclusions.'

'You didn't say that then?'

'I said that was a possible line of inquiry.'

'Is your brother dead?'

'I don't know.'

Thank God for that! 'He hasn't turned up?'

'No.'

'Missing, then. But not in action like many poor devils in Russia and one of my mechanics.'

'I have to try to discover what happened.'

'Though thousands of mothers whose sons marched off with a song on their lips can't.'

'I'm not saying my anxiety is unique.'

'Do I need a lawyer?'

'I'd just like to ask a few questions.'

He stares at Heinecke. Smooth-jawed and smooth-voiced. Jochen would love to punch his face.

'I can take you down to Prinz-Albrecht-Strasse, if you prefer,' Heinecke says.

'Can you? I wonder.' Actually, he really wonders

if he can. Attack may be the best defence here. 'Isn't your brother's disappearance a police matter? How can you spend time on it? Shouldn't you be gathering up denunciations against anti-state criminals? I thought that was your function, setting neighbour against neighbour, children against parents.'

'This is my own time.'

'Oh, a couple of days free. Nice.'

'You were seen in a shelter talking to my brother. There was a young woman with you.'

'Aren't I the lucky one?'

'Who is she?'

'Mind your own business.'

'You won't tell me?'

'Are you married? Engaged?'

'No.'

'You surprise me. Well, she was not my fiancée, and we were in a shelter in an air raid. You wouldn't expect me to tell the world who she is. I'm silent on the subject.'

'She didn't look Aryan.'

'Rather like you, then. And myself, come to that. I've got the hair more or less but I'm a bit of a runt, aren't I? Not exactly the muscled warrior type, eh?'

'Tell me who she was.'

'And drop her in the shit, too?'

'I'm making inquiries. If she's done nothing wrong, she'll have nothing to fear.'

'Have you made inquiries about your brother?'

'I'm trying to find him.'

He should stop talking but Heinecke is making him

angry. He's letting Jochen go on. Probably hopes he'll trip up, give something away.

'Well, remember this for when you start your file on him. He's a brutal man and he's twisted up here.' Jochen taps his temple. 'He thought he had some hold over my sister. He followed her to Vienna when she tried to get away from him. She saw him there and wrote me a terror-stricken letter about him. I believe he raped and murdered her and he frightened a hotel clerk into changing his identification of him. I saw him with a large dressing on his cheek where my sister injured him when she fought back.'

'I remember that. Flying glass in an air raid when he was visiting our sister.'

Jochen laughs. 'Of course, it was.'

Stop now. Has he used the present tense all the time he's been talking about Heinecke?

'I'll be back with an arrest warrant.'

'Don't you need some grounds for that?'

'Non-cooperation.'

Oh, Jesus. Time to start wriggling.

'Look, I understand your concern about your brother. I had a sister, remember, but really, you should take the time to find out more about him. He's probably got enemies all over Berlin. Find them and try talking to some of them.'

'I'll see you again.' Heinecke puts on his hat and a few steps on the marble have him at the door and through it.

'Did you kill him?' Winter says when Jochen tells him about Heinecke.

'Of course not.'

'Do you know anything about his disappearance?'

'No!'

'I'll tell Galland about this idiot.'

'Get him to send me back to Jonny Beck. I don't want to miss the big attack.'

He'll be safe with Jonny. He can rely on him to keep telling Heinecke to fuck off.

But Galland won't post him back.

'We've got him!' Bauer says, wearing a huge grin one evening when he gets in.

'Who?'

'Our blackout rapist-killer! Finally. He made a mistake. He tried it on with one of the policewomen we've had out on the streets. Great girl. She hung onto him yelling and screaming till her back-up got there.' He pours out brandy. 'Here. I've been keeping this. It's the last of it.'

But the next time Jochen sees him he's much less happy. He drops into a chair, doesn't even take his hat off. Jochen turns from the piano where he's been playing a piece that's new to him.

'What's the matter, Rolf? Did you get the wrong guy?'

'No. He confessed. Spewed it all out.'

'So?'

'He's not a Berliner. The attacks started about three months after he arrived here. He's an engine driver. About fifty. There was a shortage here, so he was one of the ones they transferred. He's a nasty piece of work. Keeps to himself. Made no friends here. Prowls about alone through the blackout when he's not working.'

'What is it you're telling me?'

'He's Austrian. He was transferred from Vienna.'

'Oh, Jesus!'

'Jochen, it's awful to have to tell you this but it was him. Before Berlin, he killed a couple of times in Austria, too. He gave us dates and places. I'm afraid Ilse was his second victim there.'

Jochen bends over and hugs his knees, stares at the carpet. Has that whimper come from him? He's learnt to control his thoughts of Ilse, move on quickly when they ambush him, but he can't escape now. Ilse! His poor darling! Some thug unknown to her! When she was terrified of Heinecke and watching out for him, some other unspeakable animal chased her into that park, tore at her clothing, beat her, raped her, murdered her!

'So, not that other bastard,' he says when he raises his head after an age.

'No. Not him.'

He killed the wrong man. Well, no. Heinecke was the right man. But he didn't avenge Ilse. He killed the man who was trying to prevent Gerda's escape, who would have brought catastrophe down on Gerda, on Jochen's head and on Jochen's family. He feels no guilt about it. He's killed many more for far less reason.

But Ilse saw Heinecke in Vienna! Saw him in a shop window standing behind her! Or perhaps she was mistaken. Overwrought. He'll never know. Perhaps Heinecke went to Vienna, perhaps he was following Ilse, but the other guy got to her first.

He prepares for a trip to the Baltic coast. He's keen to go. He hopes to slip in a quick visit to Sassnitz to see Uwe, give him some money to send on to Gerda.

In the afternoon he goes for a walk while it's still light. He passes the zoo, stares at the huge flak towers there, the guns on top pointing up at the grey sky like gigantic fingers, sees the flak girls in their uniforms arriving for their night-time duties, neat and efficient-looking, long hair braided and coiled tidily as if about to set out for a hike in the country.

They'll probably have a quiet night now the RAF seems occupied with supporting the Allied armies; the raids tailed off some time ago. The people in the street seem exhausted, heads down in the main, old men and women clutching bags in case there's something to buy, now and again, an amputee on crutches. There's the clop-clop of a skinny horse and rumbling cart wheels, the sound of a train, bicycle bells, a Wehrmacht truck, a car with a boiler on the back and in between, feet on pavements, steel-tipped heels clicking on the stones. And then, in front of him, a woman. They stop.

'Jochen.'

'Frau Hofmann.'

Embarrassment. Is she going to speak, start a conversation? Or an argument? He sees his cap fly through the front door again. It could only have been her who threw it out.

'Are you well, Jochen?'

'Yes, thank you.'

'You were limping.'

'I landed badly.'

'With a parachute?'

'Yes. And are you well, and everyone?'

'Anna is working hard. Everyone is.'

He has to ask. 'How is Lotte?'

'She's very quiet. She's very hurt, you know.'

'We would have been miserable. Her as much as me.'

'I know. I told her that. A lifetime would feel even longer with the wrong person. She told me everything you said. I was shocked.' She takes his hands, gazes into his eyes. 'My husband's… work, if that's the word for it, what he's told me before has always made me squirm, but what you said I'd truly never heard. It's unspeakable. I asked him what he'd told you. I made him answer. Your report was accurate. I had no idea. You must believe me. I'm deeply ashamed. I can hardly believe it all. It's buried in my head now. I'm complicit, of course, I'm his wife. I come from the time before the Nazis, but when I and those like me are gone… what hope will there be for us all? For Germans? If everyone is like Josef?'

'I don't know, Frau Hofmann.'

'You're a good boy, Jochen. May God go with you.' She puts her hand on his cheek.

He's suddenly anxious for her, for Lotte and Anna, too. He has a clear picture of what's to come.

'You must leave Berlin, you know. Very soon. Have you got friends in the west? Someone you could stay with? All of you?'

'My husband will never leave.'

'I wasn't thinking of him. Look, when the Reds arrive…'

'Will they?'

'They're bound to beat the Americans to Berlin. Don't be here. Any of you. When my father was killed, they rounded up fifty Russian villagers and shot them. From what I've heard, that was one of our more civilised acts out there. They'll be keen to even things up. I don't mean to frighten you but it won't be pleasant if you're here. There'll be no protection for women.'

Galland won't send him back to Jonny, tells him he's not fully recovered yet. One of these days he'll just get in his Gustav and fly back, orders or no orders. He goes to Otto's pigsty and drags him out for a drink. Otto knows a place with a piano that can't afford a pianist, so Otto plays for free when he goes there, when he isn't on duty with his *Volkssturm* kids. They have beer; there's still some left. Otto wonders if it's safe for Jochen to go to Sassnitz and see Uwe. There might be questions about why a Luftwaffe *Hauptmann* is visiting a fisherman.

'Passing on family greetings from his brother? News of Berlin?'

'Then I'm in the mix, too.'

'I could just wander along the quay, breathing in the sea air, meet Uwe by chance, have a chat. I'll make sure I'm that way, anyway, visiting a unit. They can't still be checking up on everyone with the whole country falling to pieces.'

'Kid, when people have problems too big to solve, they settle on the unimportant things they can do. Following you around might be one of them.'

Galland promises he can go back for the big attack he's planning: three thousand fighters, five hundred Ami heavies in flames. He goes home feeling more cheerful and practises the new Beethoven Sonata he's come across. No 17. They call it *The Tempest*. He doesn't know if Beethoven named it but parts of it feel like a tempest. He loves it.

Rolf comes in and sits listening until Jochen finishes.

'I don't know how you do that.'

'I started when I was six. I ought to be competent.'

'Was it your mother that got you started?'

'I heard someone play, apparently, and said I wanted to do it.'

'I had a letter from her. She's quite happy there. Wonders if we have bachelor nights out together.'

Jochen bursts out laughing and Rolf smirks.

'She doesn't know what Berlin's like now, does she?' Jochen says.

'She wants to come back though.'

'No! She mustn't!' The thought alarms him.

'I wrote back at once, from work, and said I forbade it.'

'Will she listen to you?'

'You know your mother.'

'I'll write too. I'll do it this evening, get it off tomorrow.'

'Good. I haven't told her about the Austrian yet. I don't quite know how to.'

'You must, I suppose,' Jochen says.

'It will all come out. When he's hanged.'

'Should I tell her?'

'No. Me.'

They're silent.

'Someone at work said his father-in-law had got his pills.'

'What pills?'

'For the whole family. Wife and two kids.'

'To…?

'Top themselves.'

'Jesus!'

'Haven't you heard anyone talk like that? He's not the first one I've heard say it,' Rolf says. 'People can't imagine life with the Reich gone. The shame. Nothing to believe in anymore. The rug pulled from under their feet. The Reds bossing us about when they get here. Getting their own back.'

'Doing to us what we did to them?'

'I imagine so.'

'Can't you join mother?'

'I can't just walk out on my job. There are responsibilities. I'll stay and help run Berlin until they arrest me.'

'What for?'

'I'm a policeman under the Nazis, Jochen. I must be guilty of something.'

It's impossible to go to Sassnitz to see Uwe. The nearest unit he could arrange to inspect is a hundred kilometres away. Too far just to go for a spin in a *kübelwagen* and turn up on the quayside. He could put some money in a letter but mightn't it be stolen? And anyway, really, with the state of the war, the mark can't be worth much now outside Germany. Who in Sweden would want to exchange marks for krona? And do they check on letters to Sweden? There can't be many sent. Is there any point in running a risk by posting Gerda a pile of worthless paper? Probably he should forget the whole idea. Has she got enough money, though? The thought keeps running through his mind; he wakes up at night with it.

He's waiting for Galland's order to go back to his *gruppe* when he hears they've cancelled the big attack. Not Galland, those above him, probably Hitler. Galland lets off steam.

'Does Churchill do this to his guys?' he shouts. 'Do you think Hitler's actually an Allied agent?'

'Dolfo,' Winter says, 'put a sock in it. Don't say things like that, not in front of the kid.'

Galland sits there shaking his head. 'We're fucked,' he says, 'totally and absolutely. Fucked.'

He lights a cigar. Someone sends him them from Spain. Neither of them wants one. They stink and taste foul.

'They've got something else secret up their sleeves for the units I've been saving up,' Galland says. 'I wonder what stroke of genius that will be? Something brilliant that will get the lot of them killed, I expect.'

There seems little point to their inspections. Everyone's doing their best at every place they visit. It's clear what's needed: more experienced pilots, but where will they come from? And enough fuel to allow all the new guys to train, but they haven't got it.

Jochen empties his bank account. Not so much really but handy for Gerda if he sends it and she can change it. He writes to her, too, but doesn't post the letter. Rolf doesn't know for sure if they check mail going abroad but he'd be surprised if there wasn't a section for that purpose.

Goering seems to have given up. He's not around for Galland to argue with. A guy called Gollob, a laughable name, is very critical of Galland. Gollob's a strict Nazi – Jonny would love him – and he's a pal of Himmler's. Then Jonny's shot down, a bullet through the thigh, bashed about the head, injured right forearm. He's a bit of a mess, out for months.

'Go and take over there,' Galland says.

'The *Geschwader*? I never thought I'd command a *Geschwader*.'

'Neither did I,' Galland says. 'It shows what a state we're in.'

The *Geschwader*'s back at Marx. The Ami's again. He takes his turn at alarm start, strapped in, oxygen mask hanging loose ready to clip up, hood down and secured, crackle and interference in his ears as he waits for the command to start up and go. His Gustav is in among the trees, a few metres from the edge of the wooded area, all set to taxi out and take off straight from where it now stands with rain dripping from the branches above onto the canopy and wings.

Why are they doing this still? Out of the twelve he'll lead up against the Amis, five can barely fly. They'll be fortunate to get back down again. Only Jochen and a couple of others have a realistic chance of getting a Fortress. And they'll be chased all around the sky by Mustangs. Since his return he's been up five times and got a Mustang and a Fortress.

They've lost two or three on each flight and had only one body to put in the earth, the rest are buried metres deep where they went in.

Everything feels different since his return. He's anxious. He's never had that feeling before. He's never doubted his ability before. Perhaps it's his eye. He passed all the tests, read the chart with ease, sang out the bottom line in triumph, but in the air? Others seem to spot the tiny approaching dots before he does. And where he'd always have a clear idea of what was all around him in the sky, he isn't sure that he does now. It isn't quite that he's afraid, more that he's keyed up, feels he has to concentrate where before he went with the moment, let his instinct lead him. Now? Where has his instinct gone? He's had the glory, the awards, mixed with all the clowns, as his father called their leaders, but he's still in the Big Top waiting for it to burn down. He wants it over. He wants a surrender. They'll be vanquished, captured, all their vanities exploded, but they'll be alive and kicking still and Germany can wait for what comes next, when they've all lived through the shame of what's gone on. Difficult to imagine now, but in twenty years or thirty? He'll only be in his mid-fifties. Kids like Ilse will have their own kids and none of them will know anything about the crowd of gangsters he serves now. All he's got to do is live and he'll be around to see what happens.

The radio crackles on in his ears.

He calls in. 'Red leader here. Any news?'

'Nothing, sir.'

Who's that on the radio? Some *unteroffizier* he can't put a name to yet. Perhaps they won't come today. The weather's pretty foul. Stand down, climb out, walk back joking with the guys, coffee, some kind of cake someone will have managed to make. How lovely would that be?

'Build up in Dora-Dora. Alarm start!'

He looks to the right and circles his hand to the guy looking up at him, presses the button and smoke belches out of the engine. He looks along the line of Gustavs under the trees, amongst the undergrowth; clouds of smoke swept back by the propellers. The chocks are dragged away and through the vibration he feels the Gustav swaying as it bounces out from its lair in the wood and onto the open grass that stretches away before him.

He only looks in a mirror to shave. He doesn't like the pale drawn face he sees. Or the way his cheek twitches. He pops in on the doc.

'My eye stings. Could it be the wound?'

'Could be. Bathe it in hot water. I'll find some ointment. How long have you had the twitch?'

'A while.'

'You need a sea cruise.'

Jochen laughs.

'Sleeping all right?'

'Not really.'

'I can give you something for that.'

'I have to be alert the moment I wake up.'

'I've got something for that, too.'

'Pervitin?'

'Lots of guys take it.'

'What is it actually?'

'Methamphetamine. It'll keep you buzzing.'

He's been resisting Pervitin since 1940. 'What happens when you stop taking it?'

'Who knows? No one ever has.'

'Thanks. Just give me the ointment.'

He gets his adjutant, Jonny's adjutant, promoted. He's too rigid for Jochen. He moves Scholz with his eye patch in to assist him. He likes Scholz. Scholz longs to go home and become a civilian.

'I'll get some kind of job,' Scholz says when asked about after the war. 'Anything will do as long as there's enough to live on. And I'll go home every evening after work and read the paper and eat cabbage soup, or whatever it is we can afford, and go to sleep in my own bed next to my wife.' He and Jochen get on.

He talks to Schaefer over lunch when Schaefer lands at *Geschwader* HQ out of fuel. He's done well with Jochen's old *gruppe*. Schaefer was in Russia in the successful days. When Jochen tells him about what he saw at Buchenwald, Schaefer drags his own memories out: what he saw in Russia, what was left after *einsatzgruppe* commandos had moved on – the burnt villages, the piles of bodies. Sub-human or not, the Russian peasants breathed and lived, and who would treat dogs like that? Schaefer is glad he can fight more cleanly in the air, terrible though the fighting they have to do is. He can see no way out, either, and doesn't want to be taken by the Reds. His family live outside Cologne, so he supposes the Amis or the British will get there, and things should go humanely, with laws applied. If only they could reach an agreement with the Allies and unite with them to fight the Communists! But Jochen doesn't agree. He doesn't want to fight anyone anymore.

France has pretty well gone. Belgium and Holland too. But now there's a big scheme afoot for mid-December. An offensive through the Ardennes! The brass are hoping for bad weather to keep the enemy on the ground, but anyway the fighter *Geschwadern* are to support the attack in all out fashion, bombing and strafing allied airfields, destroying on the ground the planes they can't shoot down in the air. Jochen can't pass on information to his guys; it's top secret. When he asks about special training for the operation – for new guys, in particular, who've only flown interception at altitude against heavy bombers and have no experience in low-flying and shooting at ground targets – he's told there won't be any. And no more fuel for extra hours in the air. He protests. He's told to shut up. He rings Galland, who says he's already protested about it till he was blue in the face. The plan comes from the highest level. Galland thinks the next step will be his dismissal. Gollob is pushing for it.

The Ardennes attack begins but fog keeps them on the ground. And then low cloud and snow. They can't help the panzers. But the Allies can't fly either. It's freezing. God help the infantry guys trying to sleep in shallow holes in the ground! He's tucked up snugly at night with his Ami jacket spread out on top of his blankets. They mooch around the field, sit around fires. Jochen talks to everyone: pilots; admin staff; drivers; flak guys; cooks; the men in black, their mechanics. Are they building up fuel reserves through not flying? No. There are no deliveries arriving. He transfers Jurg to look after his Gustav and all the HQ flight's machines.

He writes a Christmas letter to his mother. He imagines their women's household there, singing in the kitchen, baking, passing Andreas around amongst them. He writes a note to Hertha and Lilo, his pals since kindergarten; he can't write just to Hertha. In fact, he wonders if Hertha is still his pal since he turned her down that evening. He adds a Christmas page to his letter to Gerda but he still doesn't post it.

Promotion comes in. Scholz brings the message through; Major, to go with command of the *Geschwader*. He's now Geschwader Kommodore, Major Murville. More money but nothing to spend it on. The next day they are able to take off. No airfield attacks, though, the signal isn't given. They dart about at low level below the clouds looking for targets of opportunity: parked tanks, artillery batteries; trucks; assembled troops. There's constant flak and small arms fire at them. He expects to be hit every moment. He drops his bomb on a pair of tanks, has no idea if he gets them. He shoots up a line of trucks. He darts into cloud to avoid Spitfires when his ammunition's gone but pops out quickly because he doesn't want to fly into a hill. He lands back on the snowy field and taxis into the trees. There are many wheel tracks leading straight into the woods. So much for hiding their presence.

Schaefer doesn't come back, and they've lost nine others from the *Geschwader*. No enemy aircraft claimed. Jochen may have got two tanks and four trucks, but he isn't sure. No one is sure if they got anything. But, excitement! Several guys saw a stream of jet aircraft pass them at a hell of a lick, beautiful silver twin-engined Arado bombers. So fast! Lucky bastards!

He spends the evening on the phone re-arranging *staffeln* and *gruppen*. He's confirmed a couple of new leaders before Schaefer rings through, very late. He jumped at low level. He'll be back at his field tomorrow.

The light in Jochen's office is an oil lamp on the desk, yellow light across his papers, dark in the corners of the room. It's restful. Romantic, with the right girl there. He drops the final memo in the out tray. Nothing more to do. Not even fan mail to read. German women seem no longer smitten by him. He can't remember when the last sack of letters arrived. Surely, he's just the thing to take their thoughts off life among the ruins?

He should go to bed, but he knows his mind will be on Gerda and Ilse, and when he does fall asleep, scenes from Buchenwald are likely to fill his dreams. He'll be up at first light, though, so he has no choice, and his predictions are fulfilled.

He's barely reached the field the next morning when they arrive; a sudden ear-shattering roar and a scream of Typhoons appearing low over the distant trees, their engines shrieking as they pull up after dropping bombs on the wood where their aeroplanes hide. The Typhoons leave the pair of Gustavs that were about to take off from the centre of the field ablaze, their pilots trapped inside. He climbs out of the trench he's leapt into and watches the enemy planes, eight of them, disappear beyond the trees, finally surrounded by black bursts from the light flak that's supposed to protect the field. The wood is on fire. He gets to work organising men to wheel out as many of the Gustavs as they can manage. Ammunition in the machines that are burning begins to explode.

They have four undamaged Gustavs left from the *gruppe* based here. Fifteen need repairs, from minor to drastic. Jochen's Gustav has burnt. He gets on the phone to report his status. He's told to forget repairs. It's not worth it. Just get pilots over to the aircraft park and pick up new ones. Despite all the bombing, production has gone through the roof and they have more new aircraft available than they have pilots.

He waits till he's confident the Mustangs have stopped their roving for the day and packs ten pilots into their communications aircraft, a Siebel 204: two engines, twin rudders like a Lancaster, huge, glazed nose like a Heinkel 111. Jochen feels exposed up front but pulls rank to fly it; he's more comfortable in control. Schaefer stands at the machine gun in the roof, facing back, ready to call out Indians and fight them off. Jochen plans to imitate the British corkscrew manoeuvre if they're attacked. He's never performed it but zu Sayn-Wittgenstein described it to him, having had Lancasters escape his guns by using it. Just before they reach the aircraft park, he warns everyone and tries it out. His passengers shout and cheer.

Another Christmas. The cooks do their best, a couple of pigs bite the dust for them. Someone digs up some beer. There's a sing song. Jochen plays, of course, and mid-song he has a brainwave. Lotte's ring! No bulky bank notes to post, no difficulty exchanging them.

He adds a page to Gerda's letter: Lotte's engagement ring, diamonds, don't keep it, sell it. He writes to Uwe, explains the favour he can do for him, puts some money inside along with the letter to Gerda containing the ring and puts it in a drawer for a few days while he runs the whole idea through his mind for flaws.

New Year's Eve. Another celebration planned until orders come through: the long-delayed airfield attack. It's got a name, too: Operation Baseplate. He has strong forebodings. Only sixteen hours warning! And what about preparation? He does his best with the *gruppen* commanders – they'll have to brief their guys; maps on the wall with tapes across to mark the routes.

They have to wait for mist to clear and they take off late at nine o'clock. A Junkers 188 leads them to do their navigating. They fly in radio silence at low altitude, just above church spire height. With any luck everyone they're attacking will be hungover. He glances to each side; the sun glints off the canopies and wings of their Gustavs. It's exhilarating to fly so fast, so low, as they tear across the snowy countryside in their usual fours, two leaders, two wing men in each. The roar of his engine, distant to him through headphones, must be appalling on the ground, multiplied as it is by seventy, the number of Gustavs in their force.

After twenty-five minutes they make a turn to port, and there's the water tower they expect and the field at Eindhoven. There are Typhoons assembling for take-off, two dozen or so? Jochen drops his bomb between two of them and shoots at a couple of others five hundred metres further on. There are black bursts of flak all around them. He fires into a Mosquito parked on the edge of the field, which bursts into flames. Past the field now, he banks in a tight right-hand turn that pushes him firmly into his seat. The sky to his left is clear, the field appears to his right; blazing aeroplanes, tracer flying across from flak positions, black bursts low in the sky. A Gustav explodes in a great orange ball of fire and spins across the field and into a Typhoon, which explodes too. Black smoke rises in many places. He pushes the stick forwards and makes for a line of parked Spitfires. His shells and bullets strike the ground and march towards his targets, hitting one, two, three of them before his ammunition runs out. One after the other they burn. A Gustav flies into the ground. Two others collide and fall together. There's another to his right, climbing and on fire. A body falls from it but he's past before he can see a parachute.

He's beyond the airfield perimeter when he feels a whack under his seat. His Gustav bounces up and falls. No change in engine note, no holes visible on the wings, the controls are fine, all the dials in front of him, too. Just in case, he gains some height for a jump. There are other Gustavs in front and around him all heading the same way.

'Fourteen here, at one thousand metres,' he calls, 'form up on me.'

Gustavs turn, slow, catch up and slot into fours. Probably no one has any ammunition left.

After ten minutes, with fields and buildings flashing by below: 'Boss, you've got a trail of coolant.'

He glances down. The temperature's going up on the dial. 'Victor, victor.'

Five minutes to friendly territory? 'Keep your eyes peeled,' he calls.

An agony of tension with the temperature rising but he makes the field with the dial on maximum. The undercarriage won't drop. He jettisons the canopy and comes in on his belly down the far side of the field to keep the rest of it clear for everyone else. Ploughing through the soft earth stops the Gustav quickly. He climbs out fast and watches his guys come in. There aren't many of them.

Inquest time. He got four definitely and probably four more. In the *gruppe* he flew with, the ones who got back claim ten in total. The ones who aren't back? No idea. There are another nineteen claims from the rest of his *Geschwader* – what's left of it. Two *gruppe* commanders are gone, three *staffel* commanders missing, and twenty-two others. As the reports come in, his mood gets lower and lower. Schaefer's dead. Blew up over the field he was attacking. Schreiber got down with a bullet through his thigh. Who's going to lead now?

As the afternoon wears on and evening begins, more reports arrive. Some *gruppen* failed to find their assigned airfields. In total, 237 pilots are killed or missing with eighteen wounded out of 900 who attacked. The survivors claim 250 destroyed and another one hundred probables.

Jochen knows that claims are often wishful thinking but anyway, the destroyed claims are only what they've lost. With a third of their machines gone as well as the pilots who flew them, and such a high proportion of leaders lost, it's clear that, as Galland says, they are fucked. Absolutely. The RAF and the Amis will fly their replacements over in a day or two.

He has a rant at Scholz, poor man, who eventually says, 'Yes, boss.'

He apologises and goes to the mess where he plays *The Tempest*, very fast and very loud. The guys sit quietly and endure it. When he's finished, a few applaud but he stops them.

'I'm sorry for that,' he says, 'and everything.'

Someone brings him over a schnapps. He knocks it back and turns to the keyboard again. He plays *Schwarze Orchideen*.

He phones Winter and Galland. What's to be done? They can barely take off each day. Half a dozen Gustavs, sometimes only two or three. Even with the transfer of bomber pilots to make up numbers, the fighter arm of the Luftwaffe has almost disappeared.

A letter arrives from Hertha. Are they still friends, then? He slits it open. She thinks he ought to know, his mother's just gone back to Berlin! They tried to persuade her to stay but she was adamant. Almost trembling with anxiety, he finally reaches Rolf. The line's dreadful. She says she wanted to be in Berlin because they've caught her baby's murderer.

There's no logic to it. There's not a window left in the apartment. It's just chance that the building's still standing, there are raids almost every day, Rolf says. Jochen knows. Those are the raids he's failing to stop. He stares out at the snow on the field and the wheel tracks through it. There's ice on the inside of the windows. He's wearing gloves and his Ami jacket.

On a morning in mid-January, Winter phones. Galland has protested too much. He's gone, dismissed. Gollob has taken over.

Jochen sits with his head in his hands. How can anyone replace Galland with a guy whose name sounds like someone clearing their throat, ready to spit?

'Boss?' Scholz is standing there. 'Everything all right?'

Jochen tells him.

'Oh, my word!' says Scholz, the family man who never swears.

10

Souvenirs de Mon Pays

A flurry of phone calls. But none from Galland. He's at
home, waiting for the order to despatch himself, as Rommel
did. Winter rings. He's spoken to Krause, Luetzow and
others. They've arranged a meeting with Goering on the
seventeenth to discuss their parlous situation, to demand
drastic action. Jochen and some other *Geschwader*
commanders are welcome. Strength in numbers.

At Tempelhof, he has his Gustav wheeled through the
snow and out of sight amongst the damaged buildings and
finds a driver to take him to Luftwaffe HQ. The streets!
The mounds of rubble! The blackened shells of apartment
blocks! The dejected Berliners shuffling around on the icy
streets, hunched up against the cold, their clothes old and
shabby, some dragging little sledges with food or belongings
on and not a clean, smiling face amongst the lot of them.

At Luftwaffe HQ the glass has gone from the windows
and there's no heating in the lobby, but the marble is still

there for his soles to slap across. He's directed to a room on the first floor and walks straight in. Planks of wood that don't quite meet are nailed across the windows. The electric chandelier has survived but with only half its bulbs, so the room is gloomy. There's no heat here, either. The Führer gazes down on them from a wall.

Winter's at the head of the table, beautiful mahogany. Jochen nods to Krause and nods in turn as others are introduced: Graf and Steinhoff, also *Geschwader* commanders; Roedel, commander of the 2nd Fighter Division; Trautloft, Inspector of Fighters on the Eastern Front; Luetzow. Jochen lights up to add to the fug in the room. Trautloft goes to a telephone on a side table and asks for a number.

'I still say we should shoot him,' Roedel says.

'You know they'd just replace him and then shoot us,' Krause says. 'That's why von Stauffenberg used a bomb. He wanted to get lots of them, not just one.'

'So, what do we want?' Jochen says.

'Fatty gone and Galland in charge,' says Graf.

'And complete re-equipment with jets,' Steinhoff says.

Trautloft says a sentence or two into the phone and lays the receiver on its side on the table, leaving the line open.

'Isn't this too late?' Jochen says. 'We've all seen how many bombers come over each time, and the fighters. I feel like a fly up there, getting swatted.'

'Do we give in, then?' Krause says.

Jochen sighs and shakes his head.

Trautloft, at a window now, peeking through a gap in the boards, says, 'Limo drawing up.'

They all stand and face the door. Footsteps from a group approach across the marble landing outside. The door swings wide. Goering's chief of staff, General Koller, enters, followed by the fat man, pink blush on his cheeks, bags under his eyes, a pale blue uniform with white silk lapels. Jochen can't smell his scent yet, but his varnished nails catch the meagre light from the chandelier. Those in caps salute, the others come to attention. Two other officers follow Goering in.

'Sit down,' Goering says.

Both sides arrange themselves opposite each other at the table.

'Right. What do you want?'

He knows. Of course, he knows. Winter said he and Krause spoke to Koller, wanted him to join them.

Luetzow speaks. 'We're grateful, Herr Reichsmarschall, that you agreed to meet us. With your permission, I'd like to tell you our thoughts and suggestions.'

Luetzow slides a sheet of paper headed *Points of Discussion* across to Goering.

Goering pushes it on to Koller.

'We can still save our cities from total destruction, but we need General Galland back and we need jets for the fighter pilots. There are sixty 262s operational at present but fifty-two of them are with bomber *staffeln*. Two hundred more are stuck in railway sidings.'

Goering can't contain himself. His face is red now and there's sweat on his brow. 'But the fighter force is useless, and you are all cowards!' he shouts.

'That's an insult!' Luetzow says. 'Every day we lead

up brave boys who can barely fly and they die at our sides.'

'They're just Mustang fodder!' Jochen says.

'You! Shut your mouth, boy! You ungrateful little shit!'

'We're still flying 109s! They're ten years old,' Krause says. 'You haven't given a thought to how to counter the four motor bombers.'

'The fighter *staffeln* need 262s. It's the only answer,' Winter says. 'Or all our boys will be dead in a month.'

'Wake up and stop dreaming, Winter. You're not getting your hands on jets, you're too scared to fly them. I'll leave them with the boys who've got the courage to use them properly.'

Luetzow says, 'This discussion is pointless. Herr Reichsmarschall, there's only one solution, you need to go and General Galland needs to replace you.'

'Yes!' they all say.

Goering stands; sweat and contempt on his face. 'That's it, isn't it? Galland's behind all this and he's sent you to do his dirty work for him. This is mutiny, it's treason! I'll have you all shot, and Galland's number one! And don't bother to make wills, the Reich will take everything!' He grabs the points of discussion, screws it up and throws it at Luetzow. 'Here, keep it! I wouldn't wipe my arse on it!' He turns and stomps out followed by Koller and the two aides.

Jochen looks around at the others. He points at his temple and twirls his finger.

Trautloft stands and goes over to pick up the telephone.

'Did you hear all that, Dolfo?' He listens for a while and says, 'Yes, look after yourself.' He puts down the receiver and turns to them. 'Galland says, "Get measured for a coffin." He's done his already.'

'What now?' Roedel says.

They all look at each other.

'Oh, let's go and get some grub,' says Luetzow.

At the Adlon, many ladies in silk still shimmer in the lamplight. Part of the hotel is closed off due to bomb damage but there's still a private room available for them. Venison again, French wine – they must have shipped a lot in way back. It feels like a meeting of conspirators. Joke: a plane flies into Mont Blanc; on board, Hitler, Himmler and Goering, who survives? Germany. He and Winter describe what they saw at Buchenwald, the beech forest, where Goethe wandered, drew inspiration. They answer several questions and with emphasis say, 'Yes,' when one or two ask, 'Are you sure?' A silence falls as many of them contemplate the horrors they've just heard of; for the first time, it seems. Jochen recounts his memories of the party where he overheard a general and an *Oberst* laughing as they discussed the decision to exterminate the Jews.

'I didn't believe him,' Winter says. 'I told him not to worry about it when he came back with that story.'

They order more bottles but Jochen makes his excuses; he must see his mother.

It's snowing and the light's beginning to fade as he starts on his way home, walking with care. A woman slips over ahead of him, and he helps her up. She scrabbles after the four potatoes that have rolled from her bag. Jochen picks one up.

'That's mine! Give it to me!'

'Of course.' He holds it out. She snatches it back and glares at him. She walks away.

'Don't mention it,' he calls after her.

He kicks the snow off his boots in the hall. The only light on the stairs is the last of the daylight coming through the empty window frame. He holds the banister as he goes up. His leg is aching again after his walk home.

His mother is open-mouthed at seeing him. 'Are you ill? You're so pale. And your eyes! You look exhausted.'

'It's the new look. I've been working on it.'

It's the strain, of course, the constant whirl of thoughts, the difficulty sleeping. His face has been displaying the state of his mind for weeks now and been getting progressively worse.

'Are you hungry?' Back to her usual first question.

'I had an enormous lunch.'

'Where?'

'At the Adlon.'

'The Adlon!'

'With some fellow officers after a meeting.'

'Don't you all have fun! I haven't been to the Adlon for years.'

She'd have gone there if Lotte and he had got married.

'We'll go for breakfast tomorrow before I go back.'

'You're not staying long.'

'I can't. Mother, why did you come back? Berlin is like hell now and you were in paradise with Lilo's in-laws.'

'They've caught the monster who killed poor Ilse. I want to know all about him. I'd like to watch him die.'

'Mother!'

'Think about it, Jochen. Think about *your* little Ilse, if, God forbid, anyone ever harmed her, you'd want to tear them apart with your bare hands.'

He can't answer that. She's probably right.

'But Rolf could tell you everything in a letter.'

'It's not the same as being in the same town, breathing the same air.'

'Every time we fail to stop a raid and they sail on here, I think about you in our cellar with the earth shaking and all of you trying to stay calm. You were safe in the country.'

'But Rolf isn't. I feel guilty there.'

Later, they have a cup of soup each. The soup lacks substance and he feels bad taking her meagre food from her.

'Listen,' she says, 'about Rolf, I should warn you.'

'What?'

'He's joined the Party.'

'Jesus!'

'Jochen!'

'Why?'

'They made it plain. Someone high up sat him down and told him. There were doubts about him. They said it was sometimes useful before to have a non-Nazi around but now, at a time of national crisis, his loyalty was in question. It was join, or else. He's worried what you'll think.'

'Really?'

'Of course. He wants your good opinion. He thinks a lot of you.'

Jochen laughs. 'Will I have to be careful?'

'Don't be silly!'

When the alarm sounds, they go to the cellar. They hear and feel almost nothing. There's been no big Ami raid today and it's probably Mosquitos over again, trying to keep everyone awake while the Lancasters properly flatten another town. He knows many of those in the cellar and in the semi-gloom of the two or three candles they allow themselves, conversations begin that avoid mention of the raid.

Upstairs, afterwards, he pores through the contents of the music stool and the pile of music on the nearby shelf. There are several pieces he's never really explored. His mother's gone to bed but she never minds him playing. He puts *Souvenirs de Mon Pays* up in front of him and plays in the lamplight. He loves it. Why has he never bothered with it before?

A key turns in the lock and Rolf comes in. Jochen swings round on the stool, laughs and throws his arm up in a Nazi salute.

Rolf looks surprised but smiles. 'She told you, then.'

They talk quietly. They want to hear her step if his mother wakes and comes through.

'She says she wants to see him die. Is that possible?'

'I could probably arrange it but it's a terrible idea.'

'He'll hang, I suppose.'

'Yes, but there's a trial first. We still go through the niceties.'

'It seems ages since you told me you'd caught him.'

'They're getting the evidence together. They want a

conviction for every victim. It takes a while.'

'Can't you get her to leave Berlin, Rolf?'

'I've tried.'

'But they're in East Prussia now and there are terrible stories going round about what goes on with the women when the Ivans go into a town. I wake up in the night thinking about it, some filthy Russian soldier and my mother! And it probably wouldn't be just the one!'

'You don't need to go on. I have the same thoughts.'

'Have you told her in detail?'

Rolf shakes his head.

'You must! I can't do it. I'm her little boy. And you'll be arrested. You said so. And anyway, if you tried to protect her, you'd just get a bullet in the head.'

'You're right, of course.'

'Will you do it then?'

Rolf nods. 'But leaving Berlin now is easier said than done. The trains are in chaos. And the ones that do run often get bombed or shot up. There might be even more danger on a train.'

Jochen's quiet for a moment as he runs through the thoughts he's had in the dark of the night. He tells Rolf.

'Do you think you could?'

'I do. But I don't know when. I'd try and tell you if I can get a message through in some way or other, but she'd need to be ready. Even if I haven't managed to contact you. Two minutes when I turn up. Coat on, grab her air raid bag. No goodbyes if you're not here. Do that before. We'll have to be fast.'

Rolf shakes his head. 'What have we come to? A

thousand years, eh? They managed twelve. I wish we had some brandy.'

They plough through the snow to the Adlon. Daylight reveals the shabbiness that night and lamplight hides. The waiters fawn on him, the hero of the Reich, but they look exhausted, as if they've been up all night on fire watch. The Adlon manages some real coffee though, and his mother's eyes light up as she tastes it. It costs an arm and a leg. They find a woodburning taxi and Jochen drops her at home before he gets himself driven back to Tempelhof and his Gustav.

Smoke is rising from a column on a road ahead of him. Tanks and trucks, artillery. They must be desperate to be moving like this in daylight. Some of the vehicles are driving off the road and into the snow-covered fields to the side. Two Mustangs are lining up for a second run. The wing-man has got careless; he's following on where his leader goes. He should be higher and out to the side and only come in when his boss has attacked and is free to watch out for him. Jochen hits the wing-man and black smoke belches out behind. The Mustang turns off and puts straight down in a field. He hits the leader as he climbs and turns away, revealing his radiator to Jochen. Trailing smoke, the Mustang continues to climb and a shape falls from it. A parachute streams and opens just in time. Jochen swings round in a wide circle to see behind and clear his tail. He imagines the cheering below. He'd like to fly the length of the column and wave. But anyone could be lurking above and anyway, a Wehrmacht column fires at everything.

Fuel is very short. Only enough get four up at a time. He wonders again why they have to bother. Schreiber often leads and Jochen stays on the ground. A new guy called Peltz has managed to survive for a couple of months and seems naturally talented. He'd have done well in the desert. But Peltz is on borrowed time here. One day soon he'll just find himself outnumbered and outgunned.

Jochen sends bowsers out to forage for fuel. Scholz and Jurg form a successful pair at this. Jurg is efficient and can sniff out the likely places and surprisingly, Scholz with his eye patch is able to project an air of menace that reduces argument over their pilfering.

Weeks have passed when punishment finally arrives. Scholz brings in the message. Jochen's posted to command an airfield in Northern Italy. He has a week to get there. It's a non-flying post.

'Are they mad?' Scholz says.

'Yes. But very angry as well.' He's told Scholz what happened in Berlin. The whole *Geschwader* knows by now, too, he imagines.

He gets ready to leave with no idea who'll take over. He wonders if he has time to get his mother out of Berlin before he goes to Italy. That afternoon, Jonny Beck throws the door open and limps in. He's got a stick, and his face is scarred.

He puts an order on Jochen's desk. 'I'm back. I take over tomorrow at dawn.'

'Are you well enough?'

'Well enough to take over from a treacherous bastard like you. You're lucky you weren't shot.'

'You heard about our little contretemps, then.'

'Contretemps, my arse! Rebellion! Revolt!'

Most of the guys are a bit truculent with Jonny. There aren't many left who remember him from before. They resent having him reimposed on them in place of their boss. Jochen practises *Souvenirs de Mon Pays* and stays out of Jonny's way. He's packed and ready for departure the next day when a phone call comes through for him.

'Hey, you ungrateful little shit!'

'General?' It's Galland.

'I heard the fat man call you that. What a badge of honour! Want a new job?'

'I've got one.'

'In spaghetti land, I heard. Listen, I've got a new unit. Jets. That's my punishment. Fatty wanted me shot but Hitler thought it was a waste when the Amis could do it. I can have who I want, so I'm ringing round.'

'What about my posting?'

'I'll get it sorted out.'

'When would you want me?'

'Now.'

'You don't need a good intelligence officer, too, do you?'

'Yours? Bring him.'

'Can I bring my fitter?'

'Does he know about jets?'

'No, but he's a real pro.'

'Go on then. The more the merrier.'

'Great.'

'Is that a yes, then?'

'You bet. Where?'

'Brandenburg-Briest.'

Only sixty kilometres from Berlin. He has a word with Scholz and then goes to find Jurg. Finally, he tells Jonny the good news.

'Jets! You jammy bastard! But why would I expect anything else of you?'

Jonny lets Scholz go because then he can get his own guy back and when Jochen mentions Jurg, he says, 'He'd probably sabotage my Gustav if I didn't agree.'

Jurg gets a derelict staff car going and Jonny allows them a couple of cans of petrol for the journey. They leave immediately.

At Brandenburg-Briest, Jurg drives around the perimeter in case Mustangs spot them. Destroyed 109s, 190s, 88s, 111s litter the field. They reach three damaged hangars. When they peer inside, they see 262s, Schwalben – swallows, but with the look of sharks.

Jurg whistles. 'Oh, they're beautiful!'

He goes off to find someone who can put him wise on jets. Jochen pokes his head into various buildings, looking for JV 44, his new unit. Scholz tags along. At the fourth attempt he hears voices and pushes the door open.

'Murville!' Krause calls. 'I thought you'd turn up.'

'Welcome to the final act, Jochen,' Winter says. 'I never thought you'd last this long. I thought your mouth or your behaviour would get you shot.'

'It's never too late, boss.'

'No bosses here. Well, only one. He'll be back soon.'

Jochen looks around. There's a Knight's Cross at everyone's throat. 'Do you have to have the Cross to fly with this mob?'

They laugh. But one neck is different.

'Where's yours, Macky?'

Steinhoff says, 'It stinks too much of the turd who gave it to me. I'm not wearing it anymore.'

'Neither am I, then.' Jochen pulls his Diamonds off and puts it in his pocket.

The next day, when the Mustangs arrive overhead, there's a lone Schwalbe full of fuel on the apron waiting for a pilot and start up. The mechanics run clear in time and the Schwalbe blazes. This will happen every day. Berlin is no place to be. Galland rings around.

Before Jochen has a chance to get his mother out of the city, they move south to Lechfeld, near Augsburg and the Messerschmitt works. There aren't enough Schwalben to go round and Jochen volunteers to fly Galland's Siebel. He fills it up with anyone who wants a ride down. Only one eye but with lots of shooting experience from the last war, Scholz mans the machine gun in the roof ready to call out the corkscrew. He sees nothing, but just before they reach Lechfeld Jochen does a practice run. Dive to the left, climb, half roll, dive to the right, climb, half roll and so on. Just like a fairground ride. Cheers erupt from the cabin behind him.

Even here they're not safe from marauding Mustangs.

Galland organises a *staffel* of Focke Wulf 190s to patrol at height during their take offs and landings. Jochen watches the 190s' first take-off and immediately doubts their value. One crashes and burns at the end of the field. Thick black smoke. The others fly raggedly. They need two months more training.

He gets off on the one training flight he's allowed by the fuel situation. The wonderful view of the ground ahead, the whistling whine at start up, the slow, slow acceleration, his back prickling as he imagines a Mustang's guns lined up on him, and finally the angel's hand on his backside shoving him straight up to ten thousand metres. Below him, a patchwork of German fields, meadows and bare earth where crops will soon start, and not far away the red and grey roofs of Augsburg; distant snow-topped mountains. So beautiful.

How could this sweet landscape also contain Buchenwald?

They pick up some guys who've been flying the 262 as a bomber. They're old jet hands and pass on their knowledge. There are four Schwalben available. They draw lots for who'll fly the first alarm start. Jochen, Macky Steinhoff and Tilburg, one of the bomber guys, win. Galland doesn't draw, he just tells them he's leading.

When the call comes, they roll off and climb. Jochen glances around and sees only two others. They soon spot the vapour trails and the silver dots just ahead of them surrounded by black flak bursts. They flash past the leading box of twelve bombers and turn two thousand metres above the Amis.

They're three times as fast as the bombers so they attack from the rear to gain more shooting time.

'I'm taking the leader,' Galland crackles in his ears.

'I'll go on the right,' Jochen calls.

'Victor, Victor,' from Tilburg.

Nose down. Nine hundred on the speedo. The box leaps up at him. There's a giant fin and rudder in front, a huge red 'A' painted on the silver. He flicks up the safety and fires the guns. The tail of the Fortress disintegrates, the rear fuselage breaks off and the forwards section plummets nose first. Galland's target is falling in pieces, too. The rest of the box flashes past him. He pulls back the stick to climb and a Mustang hurtles by, and another. At ten thousand again he turns to dive and hits another tail with a big red 'A'. It snaps off as the guns stop. Out of ammunition, he stays in his dive and makes for home at nine hundred.

Galland got two, Tilburg one, that's five with Jochen's. There were only a handful of parachutes so most of the crews died in their planes. The 190s got a Mustang and lost three. Steinhoff's engines wouldn't start. Galland says they need more Schwalben so that they can all attack at once.

What's the point? The 190s won't last, then the Mustangs will pick them all off one by one as the Schwalben make their slow, helpless landings.

It's mid-March. Primroses are in the grass in the garden of the house he's billeted in a kilometre from the field. The woman's husband is fighting on the Eastern Front, unless the Russians have killed him, she says. The woman's parents keep the garden full of vegetables. He brings tins of food in a haversack for them. The father is proud to have the major staying with them. He has one arm, the other lost twenty-seven years ago in some horrendous trench action in France. They boil water for Jochen to wash morning and evening. There are two children, young, four or five, unbearably beautiful, the girl with long tresses, the boy with a severe haircut. What life have they got coming? He plays with them when he's around, shows them how to produce a tune of sorts on a comb and paper. Of course, he thinks of Gerda and Ilse constantly. At least they won't have a soldier billeted on them.

It's warm in his room up under the roof. There's a table and chair. The woman used to do her homework here in the quiet when she was at the gymnasium. He finally finishes his letter to Gerda. He has to. It's time to send it. Now or never. He wraps the ring with his last clean handkerchief. He writes a note to Uwe to explain, adds a wad of Reichmarks, too, to help persuade a Swedish sailor to post Gerda's package when he's back at home, makes a package of Uwe's letter and the Reichmarks around Gerda's letter. What are the chances of it reaching her?

In the office at the field there's a letter from Otto and one from his mother. There was a bomb very close, his mother says. They were all safe in the cellar. The building is a shambles but their apartment is just about liveable in. There's a standpipe for water at the end of the road. To distract his mind from the squalor of his mother's life, he opens Otto's letter. Willi is dead, Otto's heard. Shot in the street by the SS and left lying there. He was executed as a pervert, no need for a trial or the waste of the State's resources, apparently. A placard was left around his neck. Otto thinks someone must have denounced him. Perhaps someone he worked with. Jochen immediately imagines Lotte's father sending in a letter.

Willi had lived with the expectation of violent death for years. Perhaps not summary execution but something appalling, nevertheless. An accomplished surgeon with both Iron Crosses and two sons at the front! Poor Willi! Wearing a dress. How does that compare as a perversion with shooting people on the street and leaving them there? Even Ilse's murderer will get a trial, it seems. But not Willi. No chance to explain, to put his case. Just a bullet.

Some days they're down to three Schwalben, some days they have as many as nine. Tilburg disappears. He's in their attack but no one sees him again. Krause lands on fumes and a Mustang hits him. The engines burn but he gets out and runs. 190s chase the Mustang off. Jochen gets two or three more. He reports them and puts them in his logbook but he can't remember his score any longer. The Russians are getting closer from the east, so are the Allies from the west.

Often when he's up, he glances at the mountains. He could reach them very quickly. Beyond lies Switzerland – rest and safety. Of course, he could never abandon the guys. And certainly not his mother. He decides to talk to Galland about his plan. Then Steinhoff hits a hole taking off, smashes up and burns. Guys run over. There are enough of them there, so Jochen doesn't run with them. Steinhoff emerges from the wreck ablaze from head to foot. Even from a distance the screams are blood chilling. They carry Steinhoff away in a blanket when they've put him out. His face is an unrecognisable crimson blob. They can do nothing but pour buckets of water over him. An ambulance finally arrives to take him to the hospital. Krupinski goes there with his pistol, but they won't let him in to see Steinhoff. They have an agreement, the pair of them, in case something like this happens. Steinhoff's eyelids have burnt off, they hear. They're all profoundly affected. They sit around later, silent, each deep inside his own head.

There's really no point in flying but they do: the vapour trails against the blue, the flak bursts, the dive on the Fortresses, the broken pieces falling, a few parachutes; then the swift descent, the touch down, expecting to die. Galland is hit in the leg but succeeds in landing and gets out as Mustangs strafe the field. Someone drives across under fire and picks him up from the hole he's managed to reach; a bit of a miracle. Another miracle; Tilburg limps in. Bounced by Mustangs as he pulled out of a dive, he was slow enough to jump. He's been making his way back for days.

Galland can't fly and from hospital says he won't order anyone else to. Volunteers only now. Some pledge to continue, one or two others put a bag in the back of a 190 and fly west towards the Amis. The field is a shambles. There's wreckage everywhere; enough fuel for only two or three to fly at a time; craters all over the place, the men fill them as the light fades. The Russians have started bombarding Berlin from the east, they hear.

'It was all over when he declared war on America,' Winter says. 'We should have made a new alliance against the Communists then, us and the Amis and the English.'

Galland's idea is that whoever's left will fly their 262s to the Americans and hand them over. Jochen goes to see the General.

'Can I take your Siebel, boss? I've got something I must do.'

He tells him.

'You'll need some papers, then. The SS are busy arresting deserters, I've heard.'

'Scholz is getting them ready for you to sign.'

'What if I'd said no?'

'I'd have forged them.'

Galland grins. 'You're always good for a laugh, kid. Bring them over.'

He asks Jurg if he's got any really small tools, watch repairing type stuff.

'I've got everything, boss. What for?'

When Jurg hears, he volunteers to do the job for him. Jochen sits him down in a private corner and Jurg spreads a cloth, lays Jochen's gold clasp with diamonds and the Knight's Crosses with Oak leaves, Swords and Diamonds in front of him – the good one from Goering and the not so good from Hitler – and sets to work prising out the diamonds. Each diamond is quite small but there are forty in each cluster. Jochen imagines whoever he surrenders to will steal his Knight's Crosses anyway, but the diamonds can be his hidden away, post-war nest-egg. Jochen puts them one by one into a small bag he's sewn with his Wehrmacht housewife kit from a piece of handkerchief. He'll sew it into the waistband of his trousers later.

Jochen slides eight of the diamonds over to Jurg.

'I can't take them, boss.'

'It's only ten percent. I've got the rest.'

'But you won them. You could have been killed any minute.'

'Hans was. You kept me alive up there.'

'I let your engine catch fire.'

'Sabotage. Look, even if you've got any money, it'll be useless in a week's time. Someone will always buy diamonds. They might keep you and your wife alive later on.'

Jurg scoops up the diamonds and goes off to check on the Siebel. Scholz has got the papers ready. Travel permissions for all of them, including Tilburg, who's got wind of Jochen's scheme and has offered to help if he can abandon ship in Berlin and make his own way home from there: orders to fly to Berlin on an undisclosed mission, then on northwards, discharge papers from the Luftwaffe with commendations for meritorious service.

He takes them to the hospital. Galland lights a cigar and signs without reading.

'Anything else you need?'

'That's all, boss.' Jochen salutes.

'I never thought I'd be in a hospital bed at the end of it,' Galland says. 'Good luck in the Siebel. You'll need it.' He peers through his cigar smoke as Jochen turns at the door.

'Hey, Murville, you were always the best of us. Barkhorn and Hartmann got three hundred apiece in Russia. God knows how many you'd have got there.'

He's been phoning Rolf all day and finally gets a terrible connection.

'I'll be there tomorrow. In the morning,' he says.

'Wait,' Rolf says, 'listen—'

The line goes dead. He tries again but he can't get through.

He stuffs tins into his haversack and cycles to his billet. He puts the tins on the table and runs upstairs for his things.

'I have to leave,' he tells them. The children's faces fall. He ruffles their hair. He lays a pile of Reichmarks on the table. The father tries to protest.

'You must have it,' Jochen says, 'but spend it soon. It won't be worth anything when our enemies arrive. I'll leave the bike for you, too.'

He shakes hands with the mother and the father and to the woman, says, 'I pray your husband returns.' A pat on the children's cheeks and he's gone.

A bottle goes round in the room they use as a mess. They all approve of his plan. A couple of others are off in the morning, too. The raids seem to be petering out so they feel little guilt about leaving.

'Will we live with the shame of all this in years to come?' Krause says.

'We have to survive first,' Winter tells him.

'Of course. But when everything comes out. Those

camps. The murder there. There must be more than the one you and Murville saw and the other one Murville told us about.'

'They're everywhere, I expect,' Jochen says. 'And it was all planned years ago and put into operation. We must be blind to have noticed nothing. I have to say I'm surprised at all of you. I thought I was the naïve one.'

He puts logbooks, awards, letters, Levine's watch and his zippo into a small bag and shoves it into his haversack along with a shirt, underwear, toothbrush, comb, razor, papers, two hundred cigarettes and sheet music for *Souvenirs de Mon Pays*. He leaves Levine's automatic and Heinrich's Beretta in the armoury and says goodbye to his Ami jacket, pulls on his Luftwaffe issue and slings his great coat over his shoulder. They gather at the flight line as the light begins. He distributes everyone's papers. He walks around the Siebel to check that everything is attached. The tanks are full, and in the back a can of petrol is tied down, along with two spare wheels for a *kübelwagen*, a foot pump, Jurg's tools and anything else he thinks he might need to get a vehicle going at Tempelhof.

Tilburg will be on the machine gun: two eyes and current air experience. Scholz straps himself in at the front next to Jochen. They leave Lechfeld without a second glance and Jochen heads north-west. He levels off at a thousand metres and the sun begins to appear to his right. He looks all around constantly. He has a grand view through the glasshouse in front of him. The roads below are already full, everyone on their way west. Horses haul carts, people drag smaller carts, men and women and children trudge along.

The Siebel feels like a bus, and he isn't used to flying for so long. In a Gustav he'd be thinking about coming down now but they're only halfway. The roads west are still busy. Is the whole of Germany on the move? Finally, they reach the outskirts of Berlin and Tempelhof appears. He calls in but no one answers. The place looks deserted, wrecked planes scattered around, craters, damaged hangars, but still that beautiful curve to the buildings and that vast field in front. There's no sign of any cars. If they can't find some kind of vehicle, the whole trip will be for nothing. Over to the east, a wall of smoke rises.

The Ivans must be shelling constantly. He circles the field and finds a line he can take to land that avoids craters and wreckage. He taxis up to a hangar, swings round to face onto the field and switches off. In the silence, the distant explosions from the shelling are loud. New plumes of smoke rise from time to time to join the haze of dust hanging over the far eastern area of the city. They push the Siebel half into a hangar and scatter to search for transport.

They comb the hangars and find only a motor-cycle combination that after a quick inspection Jurg says he can get going. How will his mother like that as a rescue carriage?

Jochen and Scholz leave him already working on it while they continue to look. Behind a wrecked Heinkel 111 is a *kübelwagen* with its doors hanging open. But will it go? It's been abandoned, and no wonder. In one side there's a line of holes from probably Russian bullets that clearly went through the floor as well and, judging by the heavy bloodstains, through the occupants, too, whoever they were. Jochen runs off to fetch Jurg, hoping that only squeamishness and not irreparable damage stopped anyone taking it.

Tilburg puts all Jurg's requirements in the sidecar and rides the combination over to the *kübelwagen*. Scholz and Jochen change a rear wheel while Jurg does magic under the hood. The *kübelwagen* starts. Jurg even has rags to wipe his hands on. Jochen grins and shakes his head at him. Tilburg puts petrol in. Scholz has found a bucket and a tap and sloshes out the inside of the *kübelwagen*. It's a little better.

Scholz will stay to guard the Siebel, Tilburg will ride the bike, a reserve in case of breakdowns. The now half empty petrol can they put in the *kübel* along with their haversacks. Scholz will stay with the Siebel until he believes something's happened and they won't make it back. They leave in their own little column, Jochen driving and leading because he's the one who knows the way.

Next to him, Jurg gazes around astonished at the damage, the blackened buildings, roofless shells now most of them, and mutters, 'My God!' to himself. They weave around obstacles, stop sometimes to shovel rubble out of the road, pass people trudging along, groups of *Volkssturm* building defensive works from rubble at the ends of streets. Some of the kids there salute Jochen. They look so young. If he had time to think about it, he'd weep.

There's no sign of Otto and his troop. The sun has gone, the sky is grey, and the air is damp but it's not quite raining yet.

He pulls up outside his building. The shelling is clear to hear again with the engine off. The lime trees up the road are burnt stumps with mounds of rubble all around. The windows of their apartment are gaping holes. He runs up the stairs and rings the bell. No sound. He knocks several times. Eventually the door opens.

'Lotte!'

They stare at each other. She's pale, has bags under her eyes, her hair is unbrushed, tangled. She turns without speaking and walks away from him. He follows her into the living room.

'Mother!'

She comes out of the kitchen. 'Darling, Rolf told me, but I can't come. Look, everyone's here. Rolf tried to tell you but you were cut off.'

Frau Hofmann and Anna have followed her from the kitchen.

'You must go, Christa,' Frau Hofmann says.

'I can't leave you all.'

'Jochen, take her. She's already done so much for us, bringing us here when our place was destroyed.'

'You can all come. Bit of a squash but there's room. Where's your husband?' he says to Frau Hofmann.

'At the hospital. He's got a bed there, as if I cared.'

'Mother! Don't speak that way about father.'

Frau Hofmann sighs. 'No, Lotte.'

'Will he come?'

'Never!' Lotte says. 'And nor will I! We'd rather die here.'

'Lotte,' her mother says. 'Anna, look after your sister.'

Anna puts an arm round Lotte and walks her to the sofa.

Frau Hofmann looks at him and whispers, 'Lotte hasn't been herself recently, Jochen. The state of the war, the Reich. It's all been too much, I think.'

Jochen barely takes her words in. A room full of women. His mother refusing to come. He's anxious. He's never felt so anxious.

'You must come,' he says to Frau Hofmann, 'or she won't. I can't drag her off.'

Frau Hofmann looks at her younger daughter, Anna, who nods. 'Yes, Jochen.'

'One small bag and quickly.'

The women leave but not Lotte.

'Lotte?' he says. 'Get a bag. Please.'

'Why?'

'We must leave.'

'I go nowhere. Especially with you. Traitor!'

'What?'

'All your awards, sucking up to the Führer, pretending to love him but, actually, despising him and despising the great work my father is doing for the Reich. They should shoot you. If I had a gun, I'd shoot you myself.'

'Please, Lotte. We can talk about all this later. You can hear the shelling. We don't want to be here when they arrive.'

'The great hero! Frightened, are you?'

'Lotte, those Russian soldiers, they'll do what they like with you. You mustn't be here.'

'I won't be.'

She leaves the room, brushing past Anna on her way. Frau Hofmann and his mother come in with their bags.

'Did you persuade her?' Anna says.

'I didn't think so but…'

They look at each other. He goes to the window. Below, Jurg and Tilburg are talking to a *Volkssturm* group.

'Coming soon,' he calls down.

Tilburg waves. The constant sound of shelling.

He goes to his room, a last look around at everything he'll never see again. There's a noise from Ilse's room. A couple of paces and he's at the door. Lotte is at the mirror, brushing her hair energetically. She turns at the sound of his step. She's done something to her face. She looks more human, the bags less obvious.

'Good, you're getting ready.'

'Yes, getting ready.'

She puts down the brush and picks up a lipstick.

'You don't need that,' he says.

'I must be presentable for the Russian soldiers.'

Her voice sounds strange. Has she lost her mind? 'You said you won't be here.'

'I won't.'

She sits on the bed and clearly bites down on something in her mouth. It crunches.

'Lotte!' he shouts and jumps over to her. He's too late. She's fallen backwards, jerking around. Froth appears on her lips. Her crimson lips.

Frau Hofmann runs in, pulls Jochen away and grabs Lotte's shoulders.

'Oh, no! No! Lotte! Lotte, darling!'

She turns to Jochen. 'Do something!' But he hasn't trained for this.

Frau Hofmann pulls Lotte up into a sitting position. 'We must make her sick.' She drags Lotte's jaw down, puts her fingers in her mouth. There's no reaction. Lotte's convulsions have stopped and when her mother withdraws her fingers, Lotte's head flops to the side. Her mother slaps her face. Nothing. She clutches her daughter's shoulders and head, lays her cheek to Lotte's.

'What have you done, darling? You said you'd thrown it away. You promised me! You promised me!'

They're all there. He turns to his mother. 'I couldn't stop her. There was no time. I had no warning. I thought she was getting ready to come. She must have had it in her mouth all the time.'

Anna glares at him. 'Jochen!' she shouts. She pounds his chest with her fists and then bends her forehead onto his tunic and sobs. He puts his arms round her.

His mother has tears in her eyes. 'Oh, what a thing, what a thing,' she says again and again while Frau Hofmann rocks her daughter in her arms and weeps, stroking her hair as if trying to calm her.

Jochen observes this scene of which he is part, too shocked to speak, too shocked to move. He feels Anna's body shake with her sobs. They stay like this. He's numb. How long? There seems nothing to be done.

A car horn sounds outside. He can't move. It sounds again. He must push Anna off. There's hammering at the door. He manages to pull himself away from her.

'Boss,' Jurg says, when Jochen opens up, 'what's

happening? We must go. We're getting a crowd down there. We'll have the SS along before we know it.'

'Jurg,' he says, 'we've had… something's happened.'

Jurg follows Jochen to the room. The scene is clear from the door.

'God in heaven,' Jurg says. 'Is she dead?'

'Poison. I couldn't stop her.'

Jochen is astonished to see Jurg cross himself. Jurg is shaking his head but pulls Jochen away by his elbow.

'Boss, I know this is terrible, but we have to go. Now. There'll be a mob down there soon. Leutnant Tilburg had his hand on his pistol when I came up. Someone will grab the bike and he'll have to shoot them. Then God knows what.'

Jochen goes back into the room. Frau Hofmann is weeping across Lotte. Anna is pale and unmoving, staring at her mother's back. He pulls his mother out.

'We have to go.'

'How can we? Lotte.'

'We're causing a disturbance down in the street.'

'You go, darling.'

'I've come for you.'

'I have to stay.'

'No.'

He goes to the bed and takes Frau Hofmann's shoulders.

'Frau Hofmann. Irma. We must go. Now.'

She turns to him. 'I threw my capsule away, or I'd join her.'

'You must come. And you must bring Anna.'

She shakes her head. 'I must stay with Lotte.'

'Irma. Think. If you stay, Anna will stay. The Bolsheviks are doing terrible things. They'll do them to Anna.'

Frau Hofmann stares at him over her shoulder.

'Irma. They'll rape her. And not the once. Perhaps they'll kill her.'

After a moment, she pushes herself up from the bed.

'Lotte?'

'I'll leave a note for Rolf. He'll take care of her. He'll know how to do that.'

She strokes Lotte's face and kisses her forehead. She goes to Anna and leads her from the room. Jochen nods to Jurg who comes in. Together they straighten Lotte's body on the bed. Jochen brings her hands together over her waist. He touches her forehead in goodbye. If he'd married her, she'd be alive.

He pulls two blankets off his bed and in the living room he grabs a sheet of paper from a drawer. There's no time to pussyfoot.

Rolf,

Lotte killed herself. We have no time. We have to go. Please do whatever you can about Lotte. I'm sorry. Look after yourself,

Jochen.

His mother takes the pencil and writes something. They leave the note on the table where it's obvious to see.

Jurg leads the way, carrying the blankets and two bags and they all follow. Outside, the *Volkssturm* have been joined by a crowd. Jurg pushes his way through.

'Running away, are you?' someone shouts.

'Rats leaving the ship!' from another.

'We're supposed to stay and fight. Himmler said.'

'Get away from that bike,' Tilburg shouts. He's waving his pistol.

Jochen spreads a blanket over the wet and still bloody rear seat and gets the women onto it with their bags.

'Someone's gone for the SS,' Tilburg calls across.

'Let's go then.'

They wait for Tilburg to kick the bike into life and then they slowly push through the crowd. Hands bang the bonnet. As they get clear, a stone hits the side and then they're gone.

He glances round to be sure Tilburg is with them. When they're out of sight of the crowd he tells Jurg to pull up. He leans over and tells Anna to get down in the seat well, and his mother and Frau Hofmann to lie as flat as they can. The women obey him without a question. Their faces are blank. They're in shock. He throws the other blanket over them. Without the women visible, they'll just be three Luftwaffe guys about their business.

He's in shock, too. He says 'right,' 'left' or 'straight on' when Jurg isn't sure, but otherwise, he doesn't speak. There were faces he knew as he grew up in that crowd he pushed through. Older men and women who would always greet him with a smile. This time they just glared. Did they blame him for saving his mother? He couldn't save all of them. But what will happen to them when the Reds arrive? To the women? How many more cyanide pills are there in the building waiting to be crunched? How many more bodies like Lotte's will be laid out on beds? She hadn't been herself, her mother said. The fall of the Reich, her world overturned. She couldn't accept it. But what vile creatures urged her on! Her father probably gave her the pill. Encouraged by announcements from the beast Himmler. Should he have married her? He can't stop wondering. Would she still have bitten on that pill? He'd only have made her miserable, though. He couldn't have stood her and what she believed. He'd have left.

There's less bomb damage here. There are trees with their first leaves appearing, the odd undamaged building, a grassy area but with trenches dug across it, the boys and old men of the *Volkssturm* being busy. It hasn't rained and the breeze in his face is dry now. The airfield fence appears. Half a kilometre on, the gate hangs open. Jurg swings left and there's the Siebel. Scholz waves. He must have had an anxious wait as the time dragged on.

Now he must pull himself together, clear his mind, he must be in charge. But Jurg is already out and taking the blanket off their cargo.

'Ladies,' he says, 'we're here.' He opens a door as they sit up and Anna raises herself from the floor. 'Follow me.'

Jochen takes his haversack and greatcoat and climbs into the Siebel ahead of them, dumps his kit and helps them all in. Frau Hofmann is crying and his mother supports her. He shows them how to strap in and gets out again.

'All OK, Erich?' he says to Scholz, who's got a shovel over his shoulder. He's been filling holes in the tarmac ahead of the Siebel.

Tilburg is siphoning fuel from the *kübelwagen* back into the can. He'll need all he can get. Once he's got rid of the sidecar, he's taking the bike on from here. He's delighted to have got hold of it, he'll travel faster on two wheels than four and get across country if necessary.

Jochen and Scholz are checking the potholes when they all hear a car being driven fast beyond the fence. They hear it slow, and it appears through the gate, a black saloon. Someone's still got petrol. Jochen draws his pistol. Whoever it is isn't here to help. The car accelerates towards them and pulls up with a squeal of brakes. The door flies open and Heinecke jumps out with a pistol pointing at Jochen. He walks towards him. The driver gets out with a pistol, too, but stays near his door.

'Another trip, Murville? Put down that gun.'

'I don't think I will, Georg.'

'Who's this joker, boss?' Tilburg calls from by the motorbike.

'No one. Some Gestapo creep. How did you get here?'

'The SS just missed you. But they knew I have an interest. Tempelhof was just a good guess, you being a top flyer. I want you at Prinz-Albrecht-Strasse, Murville.'

'Have you got a charge this time?'

'Attempting to export currency and valuables illegally. By the way, I found your letters quite sickeningly emotional and sentimental.'

'You read my letters?'

'Of course. We have to preserve the Reich. And really, sending your ex-fiancée's ring for your new tart to sell! Not the behaviour of a gentleman. She must be a Jew, of course. And mother to your bastard! Well, your friend in Sassnitz will tell us everything when we pick him up.'

Uwe! What has he done?

'Now tell your men to move round to you where I can see them.'

'Stay where you are! And get your pistols out. If he shoots me, shoot him.'

'I'll take care of the driver first, boss.' Tilburg says. 'I've got a clear shot.'

'I've only got this shovel, boss,' Scholz says, still carrying it on his shoulder. 'So I'll come over to you.'

He starts to walk towards Jochen and will clearly pass close to Heinecke.

Heinecke turns a little and half moves his pistol towards Scholz.

'Well, Georg,' Jochen says as Scholz gets closer. 'Are we going to shoot each other?'

Heinecke turns back to him and away from Scholz, who swings the shovel from his shoulder and brings the back of it down with a loud clang onto Heinecke's hatless head. Heinecke pitches forwards and the gun flies out of his hand. Jochen grabs it from the ground. Scholz stands ready to give Heinecke another whack, but Heinecke isn't moving.

They all turn as a car door slams and the black saloon starts up. It swings round in a half circle and disappears the way it came.

With no other distraction to concentrate on, the shelling sounds louder.

Jochen bends down and checks Heinecke's pockets.

He pulls out a package. The one Jochen sent to Uwe and Gerda. He sees Uwe beaten up in some underground cell and guilt sweeps through him again. He pushes the package into his pocket. He checks Heinecke for another weapon, rolls him over. Nothing.

'Let's get out of here,' he says. But Heinecke is lying there helpless, unconscious. What will the Reds do to him when they arrive? He doesn't fancy the death of another of the Heinecke boys on his conscience, however much of a shit he is.

'Jurg, Erich, give me a hand.'

'He'd have beaten you to pulp if he'd got you into that hell hole, boss,' Jurg says as they struggle to get Heinecke up into the plane.

'Never mind that,' he says.

'We're the good guys, Jurg,' Scholz says, 'didn't you realise?'

They tie him into a seat with the rope that previously held the petrol can secure. Jurg sits next to him with a pistol trained.

'Who's that?' his mother says.

'I'll tell you later.'

Lotte's mother is pale and stares ahead sightlessly. Anna grips her hand.

'If anyone feels sick,' Jochen says, 'just throw up on the floor.' It won't matter, they won't be needing the Siebel again.

Tilburg waves and sets off on the bike. Jochen's given him directions to avoid going through Berlin. He'll quickly find a road full of refugees.

Jochen has to take off across wind because of the wide scattering of craters. He has a good view in front though from the glasshouse. There are large craters ahead but they're off before they reach them. It's much later than he'd hoped, and he can't believe they'll avoid trouble, but all he can do is press on. He can't climb high enough to evade Mustangs, so he stays low to eliminate attacks from beneath. He heads west to get away from Russian fighters. He plans to turn north after a while. A landing in a field near Lilo's mother-in-law's place is his probably unachievable object. He pulls off his helmet. He doesn't need the headphones, he won't be talking to anyone, and he'll hear Scholz better if he shouts.

This crate is a rattle box. It was built in 1939, six years ago; the oldest aeroplane he's ever flown. A 109 is lucky to last three months. He watches ahead and to left and right and above, sweeping his head all around constantly. He hopes Scholz is doing the same behind him. He's more on edge than he ever has been in the air before; he's never had such a valuable cargo aboard.

They pass over roads choked with refugees staggering west, humping or hauling what possessions they can. Pastures dotted with sheep and cattle lie below, woods and copses stand beside the silver snakes of rivers, the mounded canopies of the trees still grey brown or a startlingly bright green with the very earliest of their leaves. Villages, small towns appear and vanish beneath the Siebel's wings; grey roofs, red roofs; gardens, apple trees in the centres of them; churches, municipal buildings, schools, no children in the yards; empty narrow side streets and then jam-packed main routes into and out of the towns. All pass beneath him. These will be his last memories of Germany from the air; this will be his last flight, no one will ever give him an aeroplane to play with again.

Way up, way above his glasshouse, vapour trails have appeared. Mustangs will be whirling high over the Fortresses, whose gunners will be sweeping the sky for Gustavs and 262s, but they'll probably see none today and probably all get home safely.

A black burst of flak forms noiselessly to port, then another and another. He must have reached the Ami lines. He turns north, revealing the land hidden by the wing. More of the beautiful Germany he realises he's been fighting for and then dashes the thought from his mind. It's time to be practical, and anyway, where do the monsters who've been giving the orders for so long come into that thought?

Should he land or keep flying north, hoping to reach Lilo's?

'You're the boss,' Jurg and Scholz said before they took off, when he raised the dilemma he knew he'd face. They could be blown out of the sky without warning at any moment.

There, beside a road where they could sit and wait for an Ami column to surrender to, is a large empty field, slightly up hill but that wouldn't matter. Can he push his luck any further? But when he surrenders, he and his guys will be taken off and the women will be left alone somewhere they've never been before, knowing no one, still in their state of shock from Lotte's suicide. He flies on, straining his ears for a shout from Scholz or the sound of his machine gun over the terrible racket of the engines.

He glances at his watch. Another hour at least. Still no attack but he's over Allied territory, so their planes will be in transit on their planned sorties to and from their targets, not looking for German interlopers who haven't appeared for weeks. He allows himself a hope for a few minutes and then for a few more.

'Left!'

He turns at once in a dive to the left, but he can't go too far, the ground is rising. He pulls up and over to the right, right over. Is that screaming he hears above the sound of Scholz's machine gun? Below, the trees are getting bigger, he reverses bank and climbs to the left. A silver shape shoots past on his right. A Mustang. As it gets smaller ahead, it banks round in a wide turn to the right. How many more? One, at least, it flashes past above, a large 'V' in yellow on its side, a crimson rudder. Jurg falls into the seat at his side and straps in.

'Just two!' he shouts.

There are woods below. He has only one trick left. He descends to fly just above the treetops. The Mustangs have disappeared, coming round for a second try. Scholz starts firing. Jochen cuts the throttle, and the Siebel slows. Trees ahead of them are mashed by the Mustang's bullets and the Ami flashes overhead and zooms up, just avoiding the treetops.

Scholz fires again at the second Mustang and Jochen cuts the throttle once more until they seem barely to be moving. More trees mashed and this time the Ami hits the tops and cuts through them but keeps flying. Jochen opens the throttle and climbs a little. The Ami makes off west. Is that a thin trail of smoke Jochen sees? The leader falls in behind his wing-man, going west.

'No more,' Jurg shouts.

Jochen opens the throttle and climbs away from the trees. There's a town approaching, which should be Stade. He'll steer clear of it. Twenty minutes after that is Lilo's place.

He swoops over the long pale drive and then the grey mansard roof with the windows set in it, over the wood behind the house, and there's the meadow he remembers. He goes straight in. The Siebel judders and bounces and pulls up fifty metres from a fence. He switches off and, because they could still be strafed, Jurg and Scholz are already getting the women out. Jochen drops bags out of the door. Lotte's mother stares around her in confusion, still holding Anna's hand. Scholz accompanies them towards the wood. Jurg has untied Heinecke. He can just about stand but doesn't seem to comprehend German any longer. What a whack Scholz must have given him. They half lower, half drop him, through the door. Jurg stands guard with his pistol as Jochen goes back to the cockpit and retracts the undercarriage. The Siebel creaks, strains and drops with a thump.

'Sorry,' Jochen says to the machine that has brought them safely halfway across Germany. It would be treason to leave a flyable aeroplane for enemy use.

Jochen steps out onto the grass. He and Jurg gather up bags and push Heinecke to stagger along in front of them.

They follow Scholz and the women towards the edge of the wood, where a figure in slacks and a jersey has just emerged and stands watching them.

Hertha. She waves and despite the bags in his arms, Jochen manages to wave back. He just has time to take the small bag from his haversack, take his package to Gerda from his pocket, push it inside the bag and thrust that into Hertha's hands, with a plea to keep it somewhere safe, before the British troops arrive through the wood to investigate the plane that's come down.

Rifles are pointed and Jochen and his guys raise their hands. Their weapons are taken and they've surrendered. Jochen leads the way through the wood towards the house. Scholz and Jurg help Heinecke stagger along. The Tommies follow. It seems the women are of no interest to the British since they're allowed just to tag on behind. As they go past the house towards the English truck parked in the drive, Jochen looks back. His mother waves. He twirls his hand, the best he can do as an au revoir.

11

Sentimental Journey

He's held with others in a hut for airmen. It's the airfield he flew to when he first visited Hertha and Lilo to beg a room for his mother. There's the constant sound of Allied aircraft in and out. At interrogation sessions immediately after his capture, he gives only name, rank and number, but when news of the capitulation comes through and there's no one left flying that he might endanger, he relents and answers any question they like to ask; about technical matters, jets, tactics, armaments, how he got so many air victories.

The English fly them to Biggin Hill in a Dakota; Luftwaffe personnel, Rall the only one he knows. A rattle trap, no windows; they stare at each other across the fuselage. They have beds in a hut and, to their astonishment, dinner at the Officers' Mess; orderlies going around offering glasses of beer, officers coming up and talking, others just staring. A flight lieutenant approaches with a smile, red hair; Richard Leonard, whom Jochen saved from a lynching in Berlin, his uniform loose on his gaunt figure; their joint grinning delight at having made it through, Jochen versus those Mustangs, Leonard versus constant hunger, the middle European winter, marching west from his POW camp ahead of the Russian advance, boots fallen apart, lucky to be alive.

Looking around, the room is just like a Luftwaffe mess; full of loud, confident young men. Lamb chops, peas, new potatoes for dinner. Strawberries, cheese. Nothing like that since his conspirators' lunch at the Adlon. They toast the King, who gazes down from the wall where Hitler would have been. Jochen gets glares from some but he raises his glass, too. Then Rall is standing: 'Fallen comrades'. No one can object. Everyone drinks.

Later, cigarette dangling from the corner of his mouth and left eye half-closed against the smoke curling up, he plays *The Entertainer*, the tune that drove Hitler from the room at the Goebbels' party. He plays and sings *Shoeshine Boy*, with which he used to torment Jonny Beck, and wonders if he's still alive. Finally, in French, *J'attendrai*, thinking of Klaus Peter, who helped pull him out of the Baltic, and whether he managed to survive his certain stint in the *Volkssturm*.

And then Brown turns up, a Royal Navy pilot; head of a unit assessing the Luftwaffe's equipment, their final new machines. They talk in German, Brown's is excellent, about the dangers of the 262, landing a 109, the Arado bomber, the best jet they had. Outside for a cigarette in the sun, they watch a flight of Meteors in the circuit break off one by one and land, cosier-looking and far less threatening than 262s.

In the mess that evening he accompanies Brown, who sings like Sinatra.

'*Sentimental Journey*,' a voice calls out.

'Do you know it?' Brown says. Jochen nods. You can't avoid it on the wireless, on the mess gramophone; Doris Day's big hit, sung by the girl next door. A nostalgic song, full of the memories that everyone has. Guys listen quietly. Brown claps him on the shoulder when they finish.

Sudden noise and a ruckus in a far corner; everyone looks round, a few rush over, a scrum forms. One of their absurd RAF roughhouse games beginning? No. Rall frogmarches a *leutnant* out of the room, Bergmann, who's had problems accepting the defeat and destruction of the Reich; a beer too many and the resentment has emerged, Bergmann becoming a staunch and outspoken Nazi again.

The next day, their mess privileges rescinded, life becomes much less enjoyable and Jochen loses access to the piano. Rall tells him how his wife protected and then got out of the country a small group of Jews, old family friends – this was before she met Rall. When the SS finally found out, they were both for the high jump until Goering got wind of the affair and told Himmler to back off. Fatty occasionally had his uses. Thinking about that tosses Buchenwald into his mind and how Fatty got those POWs out. Inevitably, the newsreels arrive next, as they seem to every day and every night in sleep; they circle his thoughts relentlessly, seeking a gap to dart in through and he has no defence. Their captors force them to watch the flickering images, although he can hardly bear to; Belsen, the camp the Amis filmed as they liberated it. What does Jonny

Beck make of those films? If he's still alive to see them. The unblinking and beseeching eyes of those unsteady upright skeletons, naked, skin stretched taut across the bones, somehow still breathing but looking no more alive than the corpses stacked in piles a few metres away. In the dark of that room, tears course down Jochen's cheeks at seeing the horrors, though others in the audience he's part of stare stony-faced at the scenes, gasping only at the shots of German civilians being walked through the camp, shocked that people who might be their own families are forced to endure these sights.

Jochen, meanwhile, through his tears, hopelessly scans the faces for the features of someone he might recognise: Herr Gold, Herr Walter, Dr Feinstein. But who could recognise any of these pitiful, unhonoured creatures, despised by their despicable captors? Everyone must be seeing these pictures; his mother, Lotte's mother, Anna, Hertha, Lilo, Frau Deichmann. The newsreels must be all around the world by now, proclaiming Germany's shame, Germany's guilt, Jochen's guilt.

No replies to his letters. Of course not, it can only be complete chaos back home. He comes across *Stamboul Train* and tries reading in English – hard work. He needs a dictionary really but no one has one. Mainly, when not being questioned, he smokes and thinks, remembers the stench of Buchenwald, the newsreels of the camps. The dreadful horrors that he'd long ago known were waiting for the world to learn of, he already knew about! He knew what was happening and what did he do? He let Winter persuade him it wasn't his business, that he had enough to concentrate on in the air. He could have protested to Goering, to Goebbels, he met them both. And Hitler; he was in an armchair next to Hitler and said nothing. Perhaps he'd have shot Hitler if they'd called him to the *Wolfschanze* sooner, before the day of the Bomb Plot. He had Heinrich's gun in his pocket that day. But how could he have? It would have been a death sentence for his mother. And what good would a shooting have done? Another monster would have stepped up. And a firing squad straight away for him.

Jonny Beck thought the end of the Jews was a great idea. That was the reaction he'd have got from any of the bigwigs. Of course, it was their plan, the solution to their problem. He remained one of the sheep and did nothing, like everybody apart from von Stauffenberg.

There is Gerda, though, always Gerda, he reminds himself. He did that. He rescued Gerda. His mother helped, Rolf helped, Otto, Herbert, Uwe and his wife, they all helped. A long time ago it all seems when he thinks about it at Biggin Hill. He struggles to remember her then, wondering, will he even recognise Gerda when he finally sees her again? If he ever sees her again. That engaging smile, wearing his cap at a cute angle, being amusing, always beautiful. But he barely knows her. What is she really like? He liked her at the club, he liked her in bed, he liked her when he met her in the street, he enjoyed their rail trip north to the sea, liked her head on his shoulder when she slept. And the day they spent talking in Uwe's house waiting for dark, he enjoyed that. And she shot Heinecke, saved all their lives. Some girl! When the alternative was Lotte, he was sure he loved Gerda. He turned down Hertha. Was it to protect her from getting too involved with him or because of Gerda? And with Gerda comes Ilse. Reaching them is his constant thought.

The Americans drive him to somewhere in London. Lots of bomb damage through the car windows but not to compare with Berlin. He tells his interrogator about fighting heavy bombers, about fighting Mustangs. The interrogator is cooler towards him than the British have been. Jochen has to ask for a cigarette.

'220, or so,' Jochen remembers telling him when asked his score.

'How did you get so many?'

His interrogator, a major, wears no wings. The British Jochen has spoken to have all been pilots. The major doesn't believe his victory claims are accurate, clearly thinks Jochen's lying. No point in talking tactics, firepower, shooting ability, practice, superiority of machines, the absence of the Allied system of combat tours, no point, really, in talking.

He mentions Sam Levine but, of course, the interrogator knows nothing about him and doesn't believe that Levine flew into a wood and survived while Jochen was in an unarmed Storch. Doesn't believe, either, that two hundred allied airmen were in Buchenwald and that Jochen helped get them out to a POW camp. He's coming across as an arrogant, boastful Nazi, he realises. They give him a dried-up sandwich in the interrogation room. What the filling is he can't make out. They probably think they're handing back some of his own medicine.

At the POW camp they're taken to in the north, the wind finds every gap around the windows and doors but he volunteers with some of the other officers to warm up by helping with the harvest. Some of the long-term prisoners have years of experience on farms. He watches for his Berlin pal, Bert, survivor of a U-boat sinking, but without luck. From a distance they see Land Army girls labouring in nearby fields.

Gathered up by their guards for news, they hear of the massive bomb the Amis have dropped on Japan. Something unheard of. Two of them. Thank God the Reich never developed one.

'That's finally the end of it, then,' he says.

A mutter from across the room: 'Until the next time.'

Autumn in the camp, the trees barer and barer, the temperature dropping fast. They're issued another blanket. He gets involved in setting up a choir, arranges auditions and turns up some good singers.

A letter finally arrives there from his mother; still at Frau Deichmann's, enjoying a country life. She works at the hospital with Hertha and Anna. Frau Hofmann earns a pittance scrubbing the floors on her hands and knees but seems pleased to be doing penance, atoning for what she sees as complicity in her husband's crimes and especially for her guilt at allowing Lotte to kill herself. His mother hears her weeping at night. They have just enough, they grow food too, of course. They have other refugees, women and children, billeted with them in the Deichmann's large house. The English, at least, are not the Russians. Rolf was arrested and investigated but is out now and working again under the Russians. Their apartment has been appropriated; Rolf has a room somewhere. He's told her to stay where she is. She says nothing about whether Rolf managed to bury Lotte. She's heard of many other suicides in the towns and villages around them and people escaping from the Russians have told them of many, many more in the east. General Deichmann is in captivity somewhere, not with the Russians. The Siebel still lies in the meadow where he collapsed it. She asks after Jurg and Scholz and has he heard from Gerda? She doesn't mention having seen films of the camps. Perhaps it would be too much to write about? Will it ever even be bearable to speak of them? He writes back full of relief at her news, sending his love to all but with nothing to say about Gerda and Ilse, or Jurg, or Scholz. Or Heinecke. The British took Jochen away from them the day after they all surrendered. Jurg and Scholz will be in a camp somewhere, he imagines. Heinecke? Under investigation or on trial, he hopes.

The senior officer, an *Oberst*, insists on a parade every Sunday, with marching and harangues from the *Oberst* on the importance of sticking together and upholding the principles of the Wehrmacht. Jochen hates it. Look where the principles of the Wehrmacht got them all. Although still in his uniform, he considers himself a civilian now and longs for nothing better than to be back in Charlottenburg playing in a club every night as he knows he could; with Gerda there to go home to.

The *Oberst* and a few others hold a regular secret discussion group where they talk about the war and the

Nazi's mistakes. With a view to making fewer next time? Jochen is invited along and goes out of courtesy to the commanding officer. It's chiefly moaning and nostalgic reminiscence: capturing Crete with the paratroopers landing on Maleme airfield, bombarding Moscow, marching into Paris through the Arc de Triomphe.

'Did you manage to see Django Reinhardt?' Jochen says. They stare at him, but he doesn't bother to explain.

Eventually, to murmurs of agreement, someone says, 'It was all the Jews' fault, why we failed. We should have acted on them sooner.'

He can't believe his ears. 'Have you not seen those newsreels? The walking skeletons? Those ordinary people locked up and murdered or just allowed to die like that? Don't you think about that? Don't you wake up in the night wanting to scream at the very thought of it all? Don't you feel any guilt or remorse?'

'Calm down, son,' the *Oberst* says.

'American propaganda,' a major says, 'all invented and faked.'

'How do you fake a walking skeleton? The Americans had just arrived there. No time to fake anything. And I saw similar things at Buchenwald.'

'If it's true, they deserved everything they got,' the major says.

'Have you ever known a Jew?'

'Of course. And there was never one I didn't despise and hate.'

'You beast! You animal!'

The *Oberst* orders him to leave.

He stomps around the edge of the camp. Have they learnt nothing? Is it still all there? Is it still all there in Germany? When he gets back, will he come across the same vile talk and the same vile beliefs? He feels like going to the British commander and denouncing the whole filthy pack of them, but old loyalties are strong. He can't do it. They were comrades, wore the same uniform, fought the same enemies even though he knows now he had more in common with the enemies than with those appalling comrades.

Christmas. Winter. Grey skies. Snow. Ice on the insides of the windows all through the day. They shiver, do exercises, play football to keep warm though snow and ice persist. At last, spring. Primroses, the first daffodils poking up. It's coming on for a year since he flew the Siebel north. Is it still in the field with the grass growing all around it, cows scratching their sides on the tailplane, staring through the glasshouse as they munch?

And then at roll call, a letter. Written months ago. Redirected twice. There's another drawing inside, quite small to fit the envelope, a beautiful girl, not the baby she was. She has a look of Gerda about her. Gerda is fine. Prays that he survived and is well. Has she not received his letters? She's working for the family again. Ilse is very well, runs about and talks all the time, never stops, corrects Gerda's Swedish. She speaks it all day long with other children. Gerda speaks German to her, which confuses her, but later Gerda's sure she'll speak both languages, which must be good. She supposes he's a prisoner. She hopes he'll be released soon. If he wants to see them, he'll be always welcome. It's her dearest wish to see him.

He writes back at once. He must tell her he's alive. The thought that she doesn't know is a knife right through him. But will this letter get to her? What's the difficulty? Perhaps one of his others has arrived by now and he'll get something from Gerda in a day or two. Nothing comes, though.

How he aches to be free! Ilse will be grown before he meets her. He'll be a stranger. Of course, they all share the same ache, even the Nazi major, though they never talk of it. In fact, they never talk. They avoid each other. He starts thinking how to get to Sweden. The diamonds should give enough money but what about papers? Can Germans travel to Sweden? Gerda says it's lovely there. Why would they want Germans in their lovely country? Could Rolf organise papers? A passport? From Berlin? Under the Russians? He'd almost assumed he'd go the way Gerda went, with Uwe and Herbert but without the drama of Heinecke. That's a small hours of the night dream, though. He'll need a ticket on a ferry. He'll need that passport. His uniform used to be his passport to go anywhere. Will Germans receive passports? He wouldn't give himself one.

In an effort to distance himself from the past, he writes three letters explaining his situation, about Gerda and Ilse, asking for letters he could use in support of an application for travel papers when he can finally apply.

He leaves the camp in a truck at last, many, many months after sending his letters, no news as to where they're going, but in his haversack, three precious envelopes containing testimonials. Leonard describing how Jochen saved his life in Berlin, Levine writing about the events at Buchenwald and Brown, as well as talking of Jochen's cooperation, reporting on his own interview with Goering, and Goering's comments on Jochen: 'Never a Nazi, that kid,' Goering says, 'he puzzled Hitler, a terrible disappointment, a pain in the arse, only tolerated for his brilliance in the air.'

At Frau Deichmann's, at the big house with the mansard roof he reaches after walking up the long gravel drive, he doesn't bother knocking but walks around the side to rap on the glass of the kitchen door before opening it and stepping in and prompting screams of surprise from the two women that he's never seen before working at the table. He makes himself known; Frau Bauer's son. The others turn up with shrieks of delight, Frau Deichmann and Lotte's mother; Anna, Hertha, his own mother back from the hospital; Lilo, and Andreas, running around now and their hostess, Margarethe, Lilo's mother-in-law.

Long talks with his mother; walking through the wood with Hertha to see the Siebel, grass growing around and through parts of it, rusting in places, feeling sorry for it. Finally, he tells Hertha about Gerda and Ilse, telling her what he couldn't say before, showing her the drawings of Ilse. A tear or two from Hertha as she congratulates Jochen, making him feel awful.

He spends hours in the British Regional Military Governor's anteroom waiting to be interviewed along with all the other travel pass applicants. It feels like fancy dress he's wearing, out of uniform at last, and in a suit of Lilo's still missing husband that's been passed on to him, double-breasted and dark grey. It nearly fits him. He still wears his flying boots, resoled now, but his uniform trousers, worn solidly for two years or more, have disappeared on a fire, his diamonds safely retrieved first. His tunic, minus badges and especially swastikas, he keeps, and his side cap, useful in the cold with its flaps down. Eventually, in the Military Governor's office, his three testimonials do the trick. He's greeted with a smile. He must be a good German, although he's not dead.

He writes. In two weeks, there's no reply but he can't wait. A train; slow and uncomfortable; a boat, cold and windswept; passport control; customs, his diamonds, less the few he gives his mother, safely resewn into his waistband again; a train; two buses, negotiated in English to avoid using German; a finger pointing a direction, a slightly uphill tramp along a dusty road; a gate that squeaks open into a sunny garden.

He drops his haversack and jacket on a stone bench next to a door with chipped and weathered green paint whose window he peers through when no one answers his knocking; a small and tidy kitchen revealed, a table, chairs.

He sinks onto the bench and leans back against the wall. The stone is warm through his shirt, the sun hot on his face, on his closed eyelids. He imagined days like this during that winter not so long ago when he wondered if he'd ever be warm again. In times past he'd certainly have been smoking a cigarette but now he seems to have stopped. Bees buzz around the daisies in the grass. There's a pigeon somewhere and a distant engine, a truck, a tractor? Otherwise, silence. He could sleep here, except that he doesn't like to sleep. Sleep is still no refuge. He can't control his memories lying in the dark; or his dreams when he drifts off. Awake, he's more in charge of his mind but even here, in this small garden, the waves of shame sweep over him again. Will they never cease? But the sea never stops, pounds endlessly against the shore, day after day, moment after moment. What can he expect? He killed people for those criminals. He was an accomplice, as guilty as them. He deserves to suffer. He deserves to drown in shame. How different he felt, how different life felt when he first met Gerda five, or was it six, years ago?

He turns his wrist and checks Sam Levine's watch, that in his letter Sam told him to keep, a souvenir of terrible days now thankfully over. He's been here an hour. Could he be at the wrong address? He closes his eyes once more against the sun.

At the squeak of the gate he opens them. Holding the hand of a beautiful child, she stares at him, her mouth open, until she smiles that smile of hers. The girl, his girl, Ilse, still stares.

He grins, jumps up, holds his arms wide, goes towards them.

About the Author

Bruce Fellows has written two previous novels, *That Quiet Earth* and *The Best One There,* as well as plays and performance pieces for Brass Works Theatre, Theatre West and Show of Strength Theatre Conpany.